Following

Jesus' Blueprint

For Praying Effectual Fervent Prayers

Dr. Gwen E. Brannum

Following Jesus' Blueprint for Praying Effectual Fervent Prayers

Published by Gwen Brannum Ministries, LLC

Raleigh, North Carolina 27616

Copyright © 2025 by Gwen E. Brannum

International Standard Book Numbers

ISBN: 978-1-964349-09-1 (eBook)

ISBN: 978-1-964349-05-3 (Paperback)

ISBN: 978-1-964349-07-7 (Hardcover)

All Rights Reserved.

Date Published: January 17, 2025

Printed and published in the United States of America.

Dedication

This book is dedicated to eight Prayer Warriors: Evangelist A. Clark, Evangelist F. Plummer, Evangelist G. Sanders, Missionary L. Bratcher, Missionary F. Twilley, Missionary L. Ward, Mother M. Temple, and Sister N. Summers. Thank God for allowing me to encounter eight honorable women who helped to create priceless memories. Amazingly, the song that Missionary F. Twilley would often sing, "What a Blessing in Jesus I've Found," is still ringing in my soul. Also, I gladly remember how Evangelist F. Plummer prayerfully assisted with preparing me to be baptized on January 1, 1984. Furthermore, joy fills my soul as I reflect on the women of God who were prayerfully working around the altar when I received the Holy Spirit on April 6, 1984. Eight years later, in 1992, Mother M. Temple prayerfully supervised me as I prepared to receive an Associate Degree in Theology. In fact, she faithfully supported me during the graduation ceremony and prayed for me as I gave the valedictorian address.

Reflecting on the honorable women's awe-filled worship, exuberant devotions, powerful sermons, testimonies of deliverance, countless words of wisdom, effectual fervent prayers, and God-fearing lifestyles, I (Gwen E. Brannum) am honored to dedicate this prayer book to eight unforgettable Prayer Warriors.

Acknowledgment

First, I acknowledge our Everlasting Father, who chose me to be His very own before the foundation of the world. Hallelujah! He adopted me into His royal family and redeemed my life from destruction by translating me out of darkness into His marvelous light. Now that I am walking in the light of our Father's countenance, I am worshipping Him in spirit and in truth, basking in His presence, communing with Him in prayer, clearly hearing His voice, receiving guidance from Him, and enjoying where He has placed me in the Kingdom of God.

Next, I acknowledge the Prayer Warriors of Apostolic Pentecostal Truth Ministries, Inc., Proven to Succeed Ministries, Inc., and Gwen Brannum Ministries, who are demonstrating a love for the Lord and His people. To God be the glory for allowing me to work with an amazing group of people.

Preface

Since childhood, I have loved having the privilege to communicate with God in prayer. By the time I was eleven years old, I persistently prayed for the healing of my earthly father, who adopted me and two other siblings. However, the outcome was not what I anticipated. As a result, my young mind was flooded with grief and overwhelming questions.

Even after I graduated from high school, I still had questions concerning the loss of my earthly father and the events that led up to his death. Nevertheless, I prayed, and God consoled my heart and assured me that He is our Everlasting Father who will never leave or forsake us. As time passed, I still missed my earthly father. Pressing through the gloom of sadness, I continued to pour out my heart to the One who knows everything – including how to heal broken hearts.

In the atmosphere of prayer, something miraculous happened! Our Heavenly Father adopted me into His royal family and bestowed upon me the benefits of being a citizen of God's Kingdom. As a result, I received the authority, privilege, and responsibility to pray in a new dimension. Also, my spiritual adoption contains a mandate to live by the Word of God, which includes the teachings of Jesus.

This book, *Following Jesus' Blueprint for Praying Effectual Fervent Prayers*, highlights Jesus' pattern as well as His principles of prayer. Jesus' pattern of prayer is the blueprint that shows us how to approach and communicate with our Heavenly Father. His principles are the core beliefs that are used to help shape our prayer life. Jesus' principles are revealed in His examples, teachings, sermons, illustrations, and parables.

In His intriguing parables, Jesus revealed different principles that apply to prayer. For example, in the parable of the widow and the unjust judge, He taught us about the importance of persistence. In addition, Jesus used parables and illustrations to teach about approaching God as a loving Father, having a childlike trust when asking for what we need, praying with sincerity and faith, praying in private, and expressing gratitude.

Based on the teachings and examples of Jesus, prayer conferences, prayer consecrations, prayer groups, prayer revivals, and praying during specific times of the day should not be the talk of what has happened in the past but should be what is happening right now. At this very moment, throughout the world, constant effectual fervent prayers are needed.

This book delves into the profound truths of Jesus' blueprint and principles for praying, which, when faithfully followed, lead to a deeper relationship with the infinite God of the universe. May these pages serve as a reminder that our prayer-answering Father, who knows all the codes, symbols, letters, and words used to give meaning to every language, is the Master of communication. With Him, there are no language barriers, and the good news is that He finds pleasure in communing with all His children in the atmosphere of prayer.

Contents

Chapter 1

Introduction

Jesus is the greatest Prayer Warrior. Through a life of prayer, He triumphed over the lust of the eyes, the lust of the flesh, and the pride of life. From His baptism throughout His earthly ministry, Jesus demonstrated the importance of prayer. He prayed early in the morning, in the evening, and all night. Jesus also prayed during times of celebration and moments of bereavement.

At the Last Supper, Jesus prayed His High Priestly Prayer, interceding not only for Himself but also for His disciples and future believers. Then, He went with His disciples to a garden called Gethsemane, where He prayed fervently.

> *He was in such agony of spirit that He broke into a sweat of blood, with great drops falling to the ground as He prayed more [and more] earnestly.*[1]

Although Jesus' soul was exceedingly sorrowful, He prevailed through prayer.

---

[1] Luke 22:44 - Living Bible (TLB).

Even on the cross, Jesus triumphed through prayer. First, He prayed, "Father, forgive them; for they know not what they do."[2] Next, He expressed His anguish, saying, "My God, my God, why hast thou forsaken me?"[3] Nevertheless, He ultimately prayed in victory, "Father, into thy hands I commit my spirit."[4] Wherever and whenever Jesus prayed, extraordinary things happened.

Before delving deeper into the wonders that occur in the atmosphere of prayer, let us consider the words of Jesus as we pray:

Our Father in heaven: may Your holy Name be honored; may Your Kingdom come; may Your will be done on earth as it is in heaven.[5]

Give us the bread we need today. Forgive us our sins as we forgive those who sin against us.[6]

Keep us safe from ourselves and the Devil.[7]

---

[2] Luke 23:34 - King James Version (KJV).

[3] Mark 15:34 - King James Version (KJV).

[4] Luke 23:46 - King James Version (KJV).

[5] Matthew 6:9-10 - Good News Translation (GNT).

[6] Matthew 6:11-12 - New Life Version (NLV).

[7] Matthew 6:7-13 - The Message (MSG).

For thine is the kingdom, and the power, and the
glory, forever. Amen. [8]

The opening prayer for this book serves as a reminder of Jesus' blueprint for praying.

During His Sermon on the Mount, Jesus revealed His blueprint, which is often called the Lord's Prayer. Instead of memorizing and persistently repeating the blueprint, it is to be used to help shape our philosophy about approaching God in prayer. When we approach our Father, we must reverence Him for being the Ruler of the universe, who is infinite in wisdom, knowledge, and understanding. Since our Father is all-knowing,

[His] thoughts are not [our] thoughts, neither are
[our] ways [His] ways. . . As the heavens are higher
than the earth, so are [His] ways higher than [our]
ways. [9]

Therefore, it is necessary for us to gain insight from God concerning His plan and purposes.

Prayer is an essential means for gaining insight from our Father. In fact, the Master Communicator encouraged Jeremiah to

---

[8] Matthew 6:13 - King James Version (KJV).

[9] Isaiah 55:8-9 - New International Version (NIV).

pray by saying,

> *Call to Me and I will answer you and tell you [and even show you] great and mighty things, [things which have been confined and hidden], which you do not know and understand and cannot distinguish.*[10]

Likewise, our Father invites His children to pray so He can impart His revelational knowledge to us. In the atmosphere of prayer, God imparts divine strategies that enable us to rise above the frailties of the flesh, trials, and temptations.

---

[10] Jeremiah 33:3 - Amplified Bible (AMP).

Chapter 2

The Atmosphere of Prayer

As a child, I loved being able to talk with our Heavenly Father. When my prayers were answered, I expressed my appreciation to God. But sometimes I would be so joyful that I would tell my peers, "God answered my prayers." Or, when called upon to testify during *Young People Willing Workers'* services, I would express my appreciation by saying, "I am grateful to be here, I thank God for life, health, and strength. Also, I am glad God answers my prayers. Those who know the worth of prayers, please pray for me in Jesus' Name."

Making prayer requests became the closing remarks for my childhood testimonies. Sometimes my prayer requests included, "Please pray that I will be who God has chosen me to be." Or I would request prayer for loved ones and friends. By the time I entered middle school, I started requesting prayers for my peers, teachers, and situations concerning the challenges I faced in school. Whatever the prayer request was, as a child, I just believed having others pray with me would make an enormous difference.

In addition to making prayer requests, I loved hearing the saints pray. Although I knew a simple definition for prayer, hearing various kinds of prayers helped me to grasp the deeper meaning and implications of prayer. Also, hearing the saints pray trained me to recognize distinct types of prayers. Eventually, I learned how to identify the difference between prayers of repentance, prayers of comfort, prayers of confession, prayers of intercession, prayers of thanksgiving, and prayers of consecration. As a result, I moved beyond having a simple definition of prayer to properly applying the concept of prayer to different contexts.

As I grew older, my love for praying increased. Miraculous things happened when the sanctified men and women of God prayed. People would be saying, "Hallelujah," "God, I give You the glory," "Bless Your name Jesus," "Lord, I thank You for saving my soul," and other powerful praise and worship statements. While praises and worship saturated the atmosphere, the altar workers anointed the children with what we call "blessed oil." Then, we were told to lift our hands toward heaven and call on Jesus. So, as a little girl, I learned how to call on the name of Jesus during prayer meetings.

Although I loved hearing the name of Jesus in songs, poems, sermons, testimonies, and Bible verses, to me, the name of Jesus had a different meaning during prayer. Scriptures like Proverbs 18:10 and Psalm 121:2 captivated my attention. Occasionally, I heard someone using the Word of God during prayer by saying, "Lord, Your name is a strong tower; the righteous run to it and are safe. Hallelujah! During the storms of life, Lord, we are safe in You." Someone else would pray saying, "Lord, all our help comes from You—the Maker of heaven and earth."

The use of Scriptures during prayer sparked my interest. Desiring to know more, I learned how to use Bible Concordances to look for Scriptures about Jesus and the name of the Lord. The more Scriptures I learned, the more I understood the necessity of calling on Jesus, especially when I read Colossians 3:17, which states:

. . .whatever you do, whether in word or deed, do it

all in the name of the Lord Jesus, giving thanks to

God the Father through Him.[11]

Somehow, I was so captivated by the verse that I started listening to see how and when the phrase "in Jesus' name" was used during prayer.

Next, I carefully observed how the phrase "in Jesus' name" was used during other parts of our services. Interestingly, I heard people saying "in Jesus' name" at the closing of their testimonies. Elders and Evangelists would lace their messages with the phrase, "in Jesus' name." People would make prayer request that included, "Pray for my family, in Jesus' name" or "Pray for my healing, in Jesus' name." Also, I could hear the Church Mothers asking God to save souls in Jesus' name.

Helping to expand my concept concerning the name of Jesus,

---

[11] Colossians 3:17 - New International Version (NIV).

I carefully observed how the name of Jesus was being used in songs. Occasionally, during the testimony service, someone would sing:

> *In the name of Jesus, in the name of Jesus, we have the victory. In the name of Jesus, in the name of Jesus, Satan, will have to flee. What can ever stand before us when we call that great name? Jesus, Jesus, precious Jesus, we have the victory.*[12]

The name of Jesus was amplified in my mind during prayer services, revivals, conventions, tent meetings, and the list goes on.

One thing I noticed, praying in Jesus' name and singing about the name of Jesus was the catalyst for experiencing a great move of God. Even down to the last night of the year, the name of Jesus was exalted. Someone would sing, "If you call on Jesus, He will answer prayer." Our end-of-the-year prayer meetings prepared us for the fresh start of the new year. The tone of the service inspired

---

[12] https://hymnary.org/text/in_the_name_of_jesus_in_the_name_of_jesu

a sense of hope and a brighter outlook on life.

After bringing in the new year with prayer, the saints would sing unto the Lord with voices of triumph. The worship songs released a divine fragrance that uplifted the soul. Through song, we were encouraged to honor the name of Jesus everywhere we went. There is one song that is entrenched in my mind that says:

Take the name of Jesus with you, child of sorrow and of woe. It will - joy and comfort give you, take it - then wherever you go. Take the name of Jesus ever as protection everywhere. If temptations round you gather, breathe that holy name in prayer.[13]

Not only did we sing about the Name of Jesus, but the songs reminded us to use His name in prayer.

The more we sang about Jesus, the more the people of God would fill the atmosphere with exuberant praises. As the power of

---

[13] https://hymnary.org/text/take_the_name_of_jesus_with_you_child_of

God was being manifested in our midst, in the height of worshipping and praising God, we would sing:

> *I need Thee, O I need Thee. Every hour I need Thee.*
>
> *O bless me now, my Savior I come to Thee.*[14]

The service would start shifting, and miraculous things would happen during our prayer meetings. While the power of God was being manifested, the Spirit-filled believers would encourage the children to call on Jesus.

But one year, I noticed how calling on Jesus intensified. At the end of January, the prayer meeting was filled with a different type of urgency. Unlike ever before, the saints of God were weeping, praying, and calling on the name of Jesus. Having been trained to go with the flow, my peers and I called on Jesus too. As the older saints got louder, we got louder. However, in my young mind, I knew this realm of prayer was beyond anything I had seen.

---

[14] https://hymnary.org/text/i_need_thee_every_hour_most_gracious_lor

Sure enough, my suspicion was validated when the Prayer Warriors started being specific as they cried out before the Lord. During their effectual and fervent prayers, the saints were interceding on behalf of the American soldiers. People were crying out saying, "Lord bring the soldiers back home." Others were crying out, "Lord shield and protect Your people." The way the saints were warring in the Spirit helped to expand my concept about the necessity of prayer.

Praying about war was new to me, and the details were alarming. As the urgent prayers continued into February, the unusual weeping and calling on Jesus increased. This time, I knew something dreadful had happened. Eventually, the saints started praying for the children, the widows, and the family members of those who lost their lives during the war. As prayers were being offered, I thought about the children who lost family members. So, in my own little way, I prayed for Jesus to help the children.

My little prayer life was expanding past the "Now I Lay Me Down to Sleep" prayer that I learned as a toddler. In addition, I was learning how to pray for people other than my loved ones, friends, community workers, neighbors, and other church people. Praying for people who were out of state or in another country helped to expand my concept about God. Asking God to help, heal, and/or deliver a soldier oversees helped to increase my awareness of God being everywhere. Just the thought of God being everywhere was captivating to me.

With my newfound fascination about God being everywhere, I would tune in to anyone using the word "everywhere" in their prayers. Then I noticed the Prayer Warriors interceding for the unsaved souls everywhere. The church Mothers were praying for families and community workers everywhere. The Missionaries were offering petitions for orphans, starving people, homeless people, and for the strength of missionaries everywhere.

The saints were praying for soldiers everywhere. The holy men and women of God were also praying for political leaders everywhere. The beauty of it all is that the saints demonstrated the importance of praying for people everywhere. They also demonstrated the importance of calling on the name of Jesus. So, learning from the seasoned Prayer Warriors, in my own little way, I called on Jesus and prayed for people everywhere.

Eventually, I practiced calling on the name of Jesus in other environments outside of home and church. Even when the atmosphere was not conducive for me to say His name aloud, I whispered the name of Jesus. Amazingly, whether aloud or in my mind, persistently saying, "Jesus, Jesus, Jesus..." proved to be a great comfort for me despite the circumstances.

Calling on the name of Jesus, singing worship songs, and filling the atmosphere with praise were the main ingredients for every prayer service. Oftentimes, during revivals, the prayer services would begin with the saints singing:

My soul loves Jesus; bless His name. . . He is a
wonder in my soul, bless His name. . . my soul seeks

Following Jesus' Blueprint for Praying Effectual Fervent Prayers

to please Him, bless His name.[15]

The presence of God was manifested, and the saints expressed their appreciation to God. Next, the prayer leader would lead us into prayer, saying, "Heavenly Father You are sovereign, holy, and supreme. . ."

While the saints worshipped God in prayer, I could hear one of the Church Mothers quoting Scriptures like Psalm 90:1-2, Psalm 100:5 and Psalm 46:1 saying:

Lord, [You have] *been our dwelling place in all generations. Before the mountains were brought forth,* [before You] *formed the earth and the world, even from everlasting to everlasting,* [You are] *God.*[16] *Lord* [You are] *good;* [Your] *mercy is everlasting; and* [Your] *truth* [endures] *to all generations.*[17] *God* [we honor You for being] *our*

---

[15] https://hymnary.org/text/my_soul_loves_jesus
[16] Psalm 90:1-2 – King James Version (KJV).
[17] Psalm 100:5 – King James Version (KJV).

Gwen E. Brannum

refuge and strength, a very present help in trouble.[18]

To me, the Word of God came alive as the saints prayed using Scriptures.

In addition to lacing their prayers with verses from the Bible, the saints would pray using words from old familiar hymns. One hymn that helped to shape the prayers is "Tis So Sweet to Trust in Jesus." A well-seasoned saint would pray:

Heavenly Father, I trust You. . . I am taking You at "Your" Word. Lord, I am resting on Your promises. Thank You for giving me the faculties of my mind. Thank You for giving me life, rest, joy, and peace. Thank you for being with me in every situation. Lord, You promised never to leave nor forsake me. Because Your promises are sure, I know You will be with me until the end. . .

---

[18] Psalm 46:1 – King James Version (KJV).

Young people as well as seniors were thanking God for His Word and His peace.

The saints who had been released from the hospital were praising God for being the Doctor of doctors. Soldiers who had returned home were thanking God for deliverance. Others were praising God for the Holy Ghost, the activities of their limbs, for jobs, homes, transportation, clothes, food, and the list goes on. The more praises I heard, the more I believed in the delivering power of God.

After the saints filled the atmosphere with worship, thanksgiving, and praises, they would ask God to move by His mighty power. Immediately, God answered the petitions by moving among His people. By the power of God, elderly people would dance like young people. Children and young adults would be running, leaping, shouting, and speaking with other tongues. Young people as well as seniors would fall on the floor and get up uninjured, proclaiming, "I am healed."

Somewhere in the middle of prayer, the entire congregation

was enraptured by the presence of God. Even people who came to church inebriated from alcohol were lifting their hands, swaying, and crying. The altar workers would gather around the souls glorifying God and singing:

> *If you call on Jesus, He will answer prayer. If you call on Jesus, He will answer prayer. Call Him when you need Him, He will answer prayer. Just call Him when you need Him, He will answer prayer. He will hear you when you call Him, He will answer prayer. . .[19]*

The more the saints sang and prayed, the more the miraculous power of God would be manifested.

As God moved by His mighty power, the saints would use their spiritual gifts. At times, someone would give a word of prophecy or a word of wisdom. Also, there were times when one

---

[19] https://hymnary.org/hymn/YL1982/507

saint would speak in tongues, then another saint would give the interpretation. As a result, the saints were edified, and they glorified God. Occasionally, the gift of healing would be manifested.

The saints knew how to make the atmosphere conducive for a great move of God. At times, we would sing "Just a Little Talk with Jesus." By the time we got to the second verse, I could hear the saints praying aloud. As the Prayer Warriors filled the atmosphere with the fragrance of prayer, we continued singing:

Now let us have a little talk with Jesus. Let us tell
Him all about our troubles. He will hear our faintest
cry, and He will answer by and by.[20]

Also, the Church Mothers, Deacons, Evangelists, Missionaries, and Elders were in the background releasing an old familiar sanctified tone.

---

[20] Just a Little Talk with Jesus - Songbook: Great Gospel Hymns, Page Number 40, Authors: Cleavant Derricks. https://digitalsongsandhymns.com/songs/10153

The anointed sounds of singing, praises, and worship filled my mind with lasting memories. There is a special joy that fills my soul when I reflect on the old-fashioned prayer meetings that I experienced as a young person. To this day, I can still remember the comfort that I experienced hearing the saints sing, "Just a little talk with Jesus makes it right." In fact, each verse of the song reassures me that I can have a little talk with Jesus about anything.

At the age of eleven, the third verse of my favorite prayer song found a deeper meaning for me. While having my own little personal prayer meeting, I quietly sang:

I may have doubts and fears. My eyes [are] filled with tears. But Jesus is a friend who watches day and night. I go to Him in prayer, He knows my every care, and just a little talk with Jesus makes it right.[21]

As the song elevated my soul, I prayed a specific prayer with

---

[21] https://digitalsongsandhymns.com/songs/10153

urgency. After I prayed, the words, "Just a little talk with Jesus makes it right" echoed in my mind.

Throughout the night, until I fell asleep, I sang and prayed the same prayer over and over with lofty expectations of receiving that for which I prayed. The next morning, I prayed thinking to myself, "Just a little talk with Jesus makes it right." Furthermore, I visualized how I would skip, jump, and clap the moment I seen the reality of my prayers. Even as a child, I was convinced Jesus could heal anybody.

Reflecting on the miracles I learned during Sunday School gave me hope. For example, in Matthew 9:27-30, Jesus answered the prayers of two blind men. In response to the blind men calling out to Jesus, "He asked them, 'Do you believe that I am able to do this?' 'Yes, Lord,' they replied.'[22] Based on their response, Jesus "touched their eyes and said, 'According to your faith let it be done

---

[22] Matthew 9:28 - New International Version (NIV).

21

to you;' and their sight was restored."[23]

In Mark 9:17, Jesus worked a miracle in the life of a young boy. The father was calling out to Jesus saying:

> . . . *take pity on us and help us! Jesus said to him . . . "All things are possible for the one who believes and trusts in Me!" Immediately the father of the boy cried out with a desperate, piercing cry, saying, "I do believe; help me overcome my unbelief."* [Jesus] *rebuked the unclean spirit, saying to it, "You deaf and mute spirit, I command you, come out of him and never enter him again!" After screaming out and throwing* [the boy] *into a terrible convulsion, it came out.*[24]

Since Jesus answered the prayer of a father who was pleading for his son, I thought to myself, He will answer my prayer! Certainly,

---

[23] Matthew 9:29-30 - New International Version (NIV).

[24] Mark 9:22-26 - Amplified Bible (AMP).

Following Jesus' Blueprint for Praying Effectual Fervent Prayers

this miracle-working Jesus can answer a young girl's prayer.

As I pleaded on the behalf of my earthly father, I thought about how Jesus healed a Nobleman's Son,[25] healed ten people from leprosy,[26] and raised Lazarus from the dead.[27] Inspired by the miracles of Jesus, I prayed for God to work a miracle in the life of my earthly father. However, the outcome was not what I anticipated as an eleven-year-old. Trying to process why such urgent prayers were not "answered," I asked, "Did God just toss my prayers into heaven's trash can?" Although my concept about how God answers prayers was distorted, I kept looking for answers.

As I talked with our Heavenly Father, I constantly thought about my earthly father who adopted me as well as two other siblings. Oftentimes, I would remember the very day my earthly father was critically injured. In addition, I remembered the flashing lights and the sound of the ambulance as the paramedics carried him

---

[25] John 4:46-53 - Amplified Bible (AMP).
[26] Luke 17:12-19 - Amplified Bible (AMP).
[27] John   11:39-44 - Amplified Bible (AMP).

away. Sadly, I would experience the excruciating pains of grief as I remember seeing my father for the last time.

Although my mind was filled with uncertainty, I still believed having a little talk with Jesus makes it right. Yes, I still had doubts and fears. Yes, at times my eyes were filled with tears. But one thing I knew without any doubt, the Lord Jesus Christ cares about me. So, even in my disappointment, I kept praying and asking God to help me.

At times, I prayed about the mixed emotions I had concerning my first birthday without having an earthly father. On the one hand, I was sad. But on the other hand, I was glad because my birthday was on a special prayer night. To me, being surrounded by sanctified Prayer Warriors was one of the best birthday gifts I could receive. Having the privilege to sing about Jesus and call on His name while the saints were praying was a form of therapy for me.

From the age of eleven throughout my teen-age years, I noticed how praying helped to alleviate the anguish I felt. But amazingly, I went to a revival meeting one night where I received the peace of God. While I was at the altar, surrounded by "Prayer Warriors," I received the Holy Spirit. At that very moment, the peace of God dispelled years of overwhelming sadness. When God's peace saturated my finite mind and healed my soul, something miraculous happened – I gained an unexplainable love and adoration for God.

After I experienced being delivered by the power of God, I just wanted to build a deeper relationship with our Heavenly Father. In fact, my desire to build a closer relationship with God was the catalyst for starting my journey of prayerfully studying the topic of prayer. While studying the Bible, I learned Scriptures like Jeremiah 33:3. The verse gave me so much hope, I viewed it as a personal invitation from our Heavenly Father inviting me to "Call to [Him] and [He] will answer [me] and tell [me] great and unsearchable things [I] do not know."

On the authority of God's unchanging Word, I practiced calling unto the Lord. Well, God showed me wonderful things in both the natural and spiritual realm. God showed me great and mighty things concerning His Word, His attributes, and His character. As I prayerfully studied, seeking to know more about our Heavenly Father, He enlightened the eyes of my understanding and gave me the ability to differentiate between His "incommunicable" and His "communicable" attributes. The more insight I gained concerning God, the better my prayer life became.

Instead of approaching God just saying, "Our Heavenly Father" and quickly moving on to "which art in heaven. . ." I started approaching our Father as being the infinite God of the universe who is immutable, omniscient, omnipotent, omnipresent, glorious, holy, loving, gracious, merciful, just, and faithful. Next, I worship Him for being the self-existing God "who art in heaven" – ruling over all His creation. Approaching God with awe-filled worship continues to intensify my faith. So much so, I am thoroughly convinced that all things are possible with God. In addition, I know without any doubt, God is faithful.

Following Jesus' Blueprint for Praying Effectual Fervent Prayers

God faithfully answers the prayers of His people. With that thought in mind, I started searching the Bible to learn more about humans calling on the name of the Lord in prayer. Then, I noticed Genesis 4:26 informing that after Enosh was born,

> . . .*men began to call on the name of the Lord - in worship through prayer, praise, and thanksgiving.*[28]

While using other Bible study resources, I gained greater insight concerning humans calling on the name of the Lord. One thing that stands out is that after the birth of three righteous seeds (Abel, Seth, and Enosh),[29] humans moved past self-accusing and nonverbal faith to a confession of faith.

Through the verbal expression of faith – calling on the name of the Lord - humans begin to:

> *comprehend all that is implied in the proper name of*

---

[28] Genesis 4:26 - Amplified Bible (AMP)

[29] Genesis 4:25-26 - Good News Translation (GNT).

God, יהוה yehovâh, Jehovah - the Author of being, of promise, and of performance. Humans found a tongue, and venture to express the desires and feelings that have been long pent up . . . and are now bursting into utterance. These petitions and confessions are now made in an audible voice, and with a holy urgency and courage rising above the depressing sense of self-abasement to the confidence of peace and gratitude.[30]

The righteous seed learned to speak with God in the language of faith and awe-filled worship.

Speaking with our Father in the language of faith and awe-filled worship is demonstrated through distinct types of prayers. For example, Spirit-filled believers can pray prayers of intercession, prayers of thanksgiving, prayers of agreement, and prayers of

---

[30] https://biblehub.com/commentaries/barnes/genesis/4.htm

worship. Also, while praying, believers can use different postures. In fact, the Bible reveals prayer can be done kneeling, bowing, sitting, prostrate, and/or while lifting our hands toward heaven. On one occasion, Jesus prayed looking towards heaven.

At all times, God looks at the heart of an individual. When the posture of an individual's heart is right, that person can effectively pray while walking through the park, flying an airplane, driving a train, climbing a mountain, or scuba diving. Wherever prayers are offered, it is the posture of the heart that gets God's attention. Jesus said,

> . . . for this reason, I am telling you, whatever things you ask for in prayer [in accordance with God's will], believe [with confident trust] that you have received them, and they will be given to you. Whenever you stand praying, if you have anything against anyone, forgive him [drop the issue, let it go], so that your Father who is in heaven will also forgive you your transgressions and wrongdoings

against Him and others. But if you do not forgive, neither will your Father in heaven forgive your transgressions.[31]

God is concerned about the matters of the heart. Therefore, we must guard our hearts. Proverbs 4:23 states: "Above all else, guard your heart, for everything you do flows from it."[32]

One way to guard our hearts is to forgive others and be constant in prayer. Persistently praying demonstrates faith and helps us stay focused on God. In addition, we experience the reality of God's Word. Jesus said,

For everyone who keeps on asking [persistently], receives; and he who keeps on seeking [persistently], finds; and to him who keeps on knocking

---

[31] Mark 11:24 - Amplified Bible (AMP).

[32] Proverbs 4:23 - New International Version (NIV).

[persistently], the door will be opened.[33]

As for me, being persistent in prayer has resulted in me receiving answers from God, finding supernatural solutions, and seeing doors opened by the power of God.

Notice, the Syrophoenician Woman demonstrated extraordinary persistence. In her persistence, she remained humble and gave the right answer in response to the testing of her faith.

> *Jesus told her, "First I should help my own family—*
> *the Jews. It is not right to take the children's food*
> *and throw it at the dogs. "She replied, "That's true,*
> *sir, but even the[dogs] under the table are given*
> *some scraps from the children's plates." Jesus said*
> *to her - because of this answer reflecting your*
> *humility and faith, go knowing that your request is*
> *granted; the demon has left your daughter*

---

[33] Luke 11:9-10 - Amplified Bible (AMP).

permanently.[34]

When we persistently pray in faith, our Father grants our petitions according to His will. Furthermore, constant prayer deepens our connection with the boundless God of the universe—the Master Communicator.

---

[34] Mark 7:24-29 – King James Version (KJV),

Chapter 3

The Master of Communication

The One who spoke the world into existence is the Master of communication. Psalm 33 declares, "By the Word of the Lord were the heavens made, and all their host by the breath of His mouth. . . when He spoke, the world began! It appeared at His command."[35] The same command that made the world appear also encompassed a set time for the world to end. Therefore, based on the time restraints in God's command, the present heavens and earth will pass away.[36] Nevertheless, the Word of God will abide forever.[37]

The abiding Word of God regulates the happenings of nature as well as the affairs of humans. In reference to humans, the Word of God serves to regulate and promote spiritual behavior.

---

[35] Psalm 33:6 & 9 - New Living Translation (NLT).

[36] 2 Peter 3:10-11 - Amplified Bible (AMP).

[37] Matthew 24:35 - Amplified Bible (AMP).

Furthermore, God's Word serves as a tutor pointing to the need for humans to stay connected to our Heavenly Father. One of the best ways to stay connected to God is through prayer. Thessalonians 5:17 counsels us to "pray without ceasing."

According to Luke, "Jesus told His disciples a parable to show them that they should always pray and not give up."[38] When God's people cry out to Him night and day, He will respond to our prayers. Whether we are sick or well, whether we are rich or poor, filled with anguish or leaping for joy - we must consistently communicate with God in prayer.

Two-Way Communication

By God's design, prayer is a two-way conversation that consists of four components: 1) sender, 2) message, 3) receiver, and 4) response. The four components of two-way communication are

---

[38] Luke 18:1 - New International Version (NIV).

designed to work in the spiritual realm as well as the natural realm. From a natural perspective:

> *Two-way communication is when one person, the sender, transfers a message to another person, the receiver. When the receiver gets the message, they send back their response. This lets the sender know the information [has been] received. This feedback is particularly important for the business world.*[39]

In the natural world, two-way communication happens between two finite humans.

From a spiritual perspective, two-way communication happens between the infinite God of the universe and finite humans. As seen in the natural, the dialogue between God and humans needs a sender, a message, a receiver, and a response. As the sender, our

---

[39] https://study.com/learn/lesson/two-way-communication-overview-examples.html

Heavenly Father communicates His message to His people through His Word, a vision, a dream, or through prayer. When God's people receive the message, we send back a response. At all times, our response should honor the plan and purpose of God.

Responding to God's message appropriately has countless benefits both spiritually and naturally. In addition to responding to the messages that God sends to us, we have the privilege to send messages to God through all kinds of prayers. When God receives our prayers,

> *[He] always answers, one way or another, even when people do not recognize His presence. In a dream, for instance, a vision at night, when men and women are deep in sleep, fast asleep in their beds - God opens their ears and impresses them with warnings to turn them back from something bad they're planning, from some reckless choice, and keep them*

from an early grave. . .[40]

At all times, God's answers to our prayers are designed to help us fulfill His plan and purpose. Therefore, in response to God's answers, we must demonstrate faith-filled obedience and thank Him for His answers.

Whenever God's people exude confidence in Him, ask Him for what we need, and thank Him in advance for His answers,

[we] will experience [His] peace, which is far more wonderful than the human mind can understand. [God's] peace will keep [our] thoughts and [our] hearts quiet and at rest as [we] trust in Christ Jesus.[41]

God's peace helps to strengthen us to properly respond to His answers. Even if God's answer comes in the form of chastisement,

---

[40] Job 33:14-18 - The Message (MSG).

[41] Philippians 4:7 - Living Bible (TLB).

His peace enables us to humble ourselves under His mighty hand.

Yes, chastisement can be excruciating; nevertheless, we must continue to trust the Master of communication. Also, we must acknowledge Him as being the One who knows how to communicate His plan and purpose by any means necessary. Hebrews 12:11 says,

> *For the time being no discipline brings joy but seems sad and painful; yet to those who have been trained by it, afterwards it yields the peaceful fruit of righteousness [right standing with God and a lifestyle and attitude that seeks conformity to God's will and purpose].*[42]

When God's answer comes in the form of chastisement, we must remember that God is at work within us.

One of the greatest benefits of having God working within

---

[42] Hebrews 12:11 - Amplified Bible (AMP).

us is being strengthened, energized, and conformed to live according to the plan and purpose God has for us. Philippians 2:13 puts it like this,

> . . . *it is not* our *strength, but it is God who is effectively at work in [us], both to will and to work that is, strengthening, energizing, and creating in [us] the longing and the ability to fulfill [our] purpose for His good pleasure.*[43]

God provides the necessary strength for us to ". . . prove what is that good, and acceptable, and perfect, will of God."[44]

Receiving strength from God to fulfill His will requires a life of prayer. Prayer is the meeting place where God reveals His plan and purpose. Prayer is also a meeting place where we seek guidance from God. For example, you can pray and ask God for directions.

---

[43] Philippians 2:13 - Amplified Bible (AMP).

[44] Romans 12:2 - King James Version (KJV).

Then, God responds to your prayer, reveals the exact destination, and assures you that you will reach the location. However, He does not tell you everything that will happen in the process of getting to your destination.

God does not withhold information to frustrate our patience or to confuse us. At all times, our Father tells us just enough to inspire hope. So, when God promise to take us to a specific destination, the proper response to His promise is to exude hope. The moment hope arises, it becomes one of the driving forces for our faith.

> *What is faith? It is the confident assurance that something we want is going to happen. It is [certain] that what we hope for is waiting for us, even though we cannot see it up ahead.*[45]

Genuine faith compels us to stay on the path that leads to our God-

---

[45] Hebrews 11:1 - Living Bible (TLB).

appointed destination.

Wherever God is taking you, He wants you to be actively engaged in the process of getting to the promised destination. One thing that is for sure, if God has revealed an exact location and has assured you that you will reach the destination – it shall happen. Despite the challenges that you may encounter, God cannot lie. Wherever you are headed, if you are traveling with Jesus, there is absolutely nothing that can stop you from reaching your destination.

On one occasion, Jesus said to His disciples, "Let us go over to the other side [of the Sea of Galilee]."[46] As seen in the text, the destination is revealed. However, Jesus did not tell His disciples about the storm that would take place during their journey. He was setting the stage to reveal more of Himself to His disciples. Amid the raging storm, the disciples had an opportunity to see Jesus demonstrate His authority over nature.

---

[46] Mark 4:35 - Amplified Bible (AMP).

Gwen E. Brannum

Although the storm did not catch Jesus by surprise, His disciples were caught off guard. As the story unfolds,

> *the storm arose and the waves beat into the ship, so that it was now full. And [Jesus] was in the hinder part of the ship, asleep on a pillow: and they awake Him, and say unto Him, Master, carest thou not that we perish?*[47]

At all times, in every season of life, Jesus cares about what we are confronted with.

Just in case you are feeling abandon upon the restless sea of time, take heart, look unto Jesus and cast "all your cares upon him; for He careth for you."[48] Furthermore, He knows what to do when the storms of life are raging. As seen in Mark 4:39-41,

> *Jesus stood up and commanded the wind, "Be*

---

[47] Mark 4:37-38 - King James Version (KJV).

[48] 1 Peter 5:7 - King James Version (KJV).

quiet!" and He said to the waves, "Be still!" The

wind died down, and there was a great calm. Then

Jesus said to His disciples, "Why are you frightened?

Do you still have no faith?" But they were terribly

afraid and began to say to one another, "Who is this

man? Even the wind and the waves obey Him!"[49]

At that very moment, Jesus showed the disciples that even the worst storm cannot reverse the plan of God. Any time Jesus says, "Let us go to the other side," His Words are irreversible!

---

[49] Mark 4:39-41 - Good News Translation (GNT).

Chapter 4
God's Unchanging Word

The immutable Word of God is a stable foundation in a constantly changing world. The principles revealed in the Bible relate to every generation, every dispensation, every gender, and every personality type. The Word of God provides profound answers to help guide us through the challenging seasons of life. The Word of God is also the basis of our faith. Romans 10:17 informs, ". . .faith comes by hearing, and hearing by the word of God."

From the king's palace to the pauper's hovel, God's Word brings life into perspective and straighten distorted views. Without the permission of finite humans, God's Word is a vibrant part of our private and public life. In fact, the unchanging Word of God influences every aspect of human existence. If we desire to grow spiritually, we must live according to the Word of God.

It is written and forever remains written, 'Man shall not live by bread alone, but by every word that comes

Following Jesus' Blueprint for Praying Effectual Fervent Prayers

out of the mouth of God. [50]

Living by the immutable Word of God is the key to experiencing spiritual maturity.

Today, countless people are living by everything but the Word of God. People are shamelessly fulfilling "the lust and sensual craving of the flesh and the lust and longing of the eyes and the boastful pride of life."[51] Despite the ungodly lifestyles that are being openly promoted on the stage, on television, and on the printed page, God's Word will never change. God's Word councils us to put "on the Lord Jesus Christ, and make not provision for the flesh, to fulfil the lusts thereof."[52]

When a person puts on Christ, that person understands the importance of communicating with God. On the other hand, refusing

---

[50] Matthew 4:4 - Darby Translation (DARBY).

[51] 1 John 2:16 - Amplified Bible (AMP).

[52] Romans 13:14 - King James Version (KJV).

to put on the Lord Jesus Christ, people ignore the necessity of building a relationship with the infinite God of the universe. Sadly, instead of communicating with our Creator, people choose to communicate with the forces of darkness. As a result, they are,

> *without natural [human] affection (callous and inhuman), relentless. . .; [they are] slanderers (false accusers, troublemakers), intemperate and loose in morals and conduct, uncontrolled and fierce, haters of good. [They are] treacherous [betrayers], rash, [and] inflated with self-conceit. [They are] lovers of sensual pleasures and vain amusements more than and rather than lovers of God.*[53]

As seen in God's Word, the failure to communicate with God leads to corruption.

To victoriously triumph over the works of the flesh, we must

---

[53] 2 Timothy 3:3-4 - Amplified Bible, Classic Edition (AMPC).

live by every Word that comes out of the mouth of God. Although the Word of God will challenge our intellect, we must resist the propensity to seek out bombastic teachers and corrupt religious leaders who uphold wickedness. Throughout the world, they are known for twisting the truth and promoting ungodly lifestyles. They are the type that can be paid to say anything to help promote and/or cover up corruption.

Ironically, there are religious leaders who have joined the forces of darkness. They are wolves in sheep's clothing - calling "right" wrong and calling "wrong" – right. While perpetuating their distorted views, they plot to silence anyone who "[cries] aloud, [sparing not, lifting up their voice] like a trumpet, and [showing God's] people their transgression . . ."[54] Nevertheless, God's Word is still going forth. God's Word will always take precedence over the ideologies of self-important preachers and contaminated teachers. The undisputable Word of God supersedes the cultic ideas

---

[54] Isaiah 58:1 - King James Version (KJV).

of the New Age Movement.

Everything God declared in eternity to be right for this day and time is still right. Everything that was once detrimental to true spirituality is still detrimental. The Word of God is conclusive, perfect, and settled. No one can ever change the authority of God's Word. The most articulate teacher, preacher, prophet, apostle, pastor, or evangelist will never be able to change the validity of God's unchanging Word. When the last skeptic pronounces his last doubts and fades from the scene, the Word of God will remain. Furthermore, when the last false prophet has prophesied his last lie, the Word of God will still be true and full of living power.

Spoken or written, "whatever God says to us is full of living power. . ."[55] Testifying to the living power of His own Word, God said:

As the rain and the snow come down from heaven,

---

[55] Hebrews 4:12 - Living Bible (TLB).

and do not return to it without watering the earth and making it bud and flourish, so that it yields seed for the Sower and bread for the eater, so is my Word that goes out from my mouth: It will not return to me empty, but will accomplish what I desire and achieve the purpose for which I sent it.[56]

Although Israel was in captivity due to their idolatry and disobedience, God gave the captive a reason to expect a brighter future.

God also communicated precise steps for starting the journey to a brighter future. The first step is the prayer of repentance. From a biblical perspective, repentance is more than saying sorry. In other words, true repentance is not just an apologetic confession or a ritual of speaking empty words to appease God. As explained in Isaiah 55:6-7, true repentance entails:

---

[56] Isaiah 55:10-11 - New International Version (NIV).

Gwen E. Brannum

[Seeking] the Lord while He may be found; [calling]

on Him while He is near. [The wicked must] forsake

their ways and the unrighteous their thoughts. [They

must] turn to the Lord, and He will have mercy on

them, . . . [they must also turn] to our God, for He

will freely pardon.[57]

God is still in the business of showing mercy and freely forgiving those who repent and prayerfully seek Him.

Even after we receive forgiveness, we must continue to seek God based on the guidelines that are provided in His Word. Constantly seeking the Lord empowers us to resist the propensity to lean to our own understanding. The snare of leaning to our own understanding leads to making provisions for the flesh and fulfilling the lust there of. The Word of God says, ". . . when lust hath conceived, it bringeth forth sin: and sin, when it is finished, bringeth

---

[57] Isaiah 55:6-7 - New International Version (NIV).

Following Jesus' Blueprint for Praying Effectual Fervent Prayers

forth death."[58] But God does not want us to perish.

Whatever the temptation may be, God knows all about our weaknesses. He even made sure we had a record of how He deals with sinful humans. Notice, in the first chapter of Isaiah, the Master of Communication is seen speaking to:

> *A people loaded down with wickedness - with sin,*
> *with injustice, with wrongdoing, offspring of*
> *evildoers, sons who behave corruptly! They have*
> *abandoned (rejected) the Lord, they have despised*
> *the Holy One of Israel - provoking Him to anger, they*
> *have turned away from Him. . . From the sole of the*
> *foot even to the head there is nothing healthy in the*
> *nation's body, only bruises, welts, and raw wounds,*
> *not pressed out or bandaged, nor softened with oil as*
> *a remedy. [Their] land lies desolate because of*

---

[58] James 1:15 - King James Version (KJV).

[their] disobedience. . .[59]

Nevertheless, God still wanted to communicate with a group of people who refused to fulfill His plan and purpose.

Although God hated the hypocrisy of Israel's New Moon festivals and their appointed feast, He was willing to forgive His people. So much so, in Isaiah 1:18-20, He said:

> *Come now, and let us reason together, . . . Though your sins are like scarlet, they shall be as white as snow; though they are red like crimson, they shall be like wool. If you are willing and obedient, you shall eat the best of the land; but if you refuse and rebel, you shall be devoured by the sword. For the mouth of the Lord has spoken.[60]*

All because of God's loving kindness, He relentlessly

---

[59] Isaiah 1:4, 6-7 - Amplified Bible (AMP).

[60] Isaiah 1:18-20 - Amplified Bible (AMP).

Following Jesus' Blueprint for Praying Effectual Fervent Prayers

communicated with people who were saturated with sin.

Throughout the Bible, God shows His relentless desire to communicate with humans on all levels in society. Communication is embedded in the eternal plan of God. In fact, God reveals His plan, purposes, and promises through communication. Even before the creation of humans, God conveyed His plan and purposes concerning His people. As seen in Genesis 1:26-27:

> *God said, "Let us make human beings in our image, to be like us. They will reign over the fish in the sea, the birds in the sky, the livestock, all the animals on the earth, and the small animals that scurry along the ground." So, God created human beings in His own image. In the image of God, He created them; male and female He created them.*[61]

Just as He intended, God created humans to be His image bearers.

---

[61] Genesis 1:26-27- New Living Translation (NLT).

Gwen E. Brannum

As image bearers of God, humans were given precise instructions describing their responsibilities, freedom, limitations, and the penalty for violating the boundary He had set. Watch the process,

> . . .*the Lord God took the man [He had made] and settled him in the Garden of Eden to cultivate and keep it. [Next], the Lord God commanded the man, saying, "You may freely (unconditionally) eat [the fruit] from every tree of the garden; but [only] from the tree of the knowledge (recognition) of good and evil you shall not eat, otherwise on the day that you eat from it, you shall most certainly die [because of your disobedience]."*[62]

God clearly communicated His plan to Adam.

Although God started communicating directly to Adam,

---

[62] Genesis 2:15-17 - Amplified Bible (AMP).

before the end of the day, He created Eve and included her in the conversation. While speaking to Adam and Eve, God communicated His plan concerning humans having dominion upon the earth. Genesis 1:28-30 reveal:

> *God blessed them and said to them, "Be fruitful and increase in number; fill the earth and subdue it. Rule over the fish in the sea and the birds in the sky and over every living creature that moves on the ground." Then God said, "I give you every seed-bearing plant on the face of the whole earth and every tree that has fruit with seed in it. They will be yours for food. . .* [63]

When God communicated His plan to Adam and Eve, He opened the line of communication between Him and the humans He created.

---

[63] Genesis 1:28-30 – King James Version (KJV).

55

Chapter 5

Created to Communicate

The Master of communication equipped humans with everything they need to communicate. In His infinite wisdom, He designed the human brain with a frontal lobe for complex decision-making and a hippocampus for memory formation. Furthermore, God designed the intricate details of every complex network of neurons within the brain to process information and form thoughts. Adam and Eve were the first humans to use the mechanisms of the human brain.

By God's design, Adam and Eve enjoyed the purest form of memory, cognition, and creativity. With a perfectly designed brain, a pure mind, and being spiritually connected to God, Adam and Eve had an exceptional awareness of God. They were thoroughly aware of God's presence as well as His voice. Being fearfully and wonderfully made, Adam and Eve also had the ability to properly respond to the voice of God. In addition to gifting humans with a brain, the Master of communication created humans with a mind, free will, and emotions.

Furthermore, God created humans with vocal apparatuses, which includes the lungs for airflow, the larynx with vocal folds, the pharynx, the mouth cavity with the tongue, lips, teeth, and palate. In His infinite wisdom, God designed humans' vocal mechanisms to work together to produce spoken language through a process of phonation and articulation for communication. While all the apparatuses for speech are important, it is worth noting:

> ... the 'tongue' refers to speech and communication. It [stands for] the ability to articulate thoughts and emotions, a gift granted to humanity to interact and express. Historically, language and communication

have played pivotal roles in shaping societies.[64]

Likewise, communicating with God plays a vital role in shaping every aspect of our lives.

Communicating with God regularly is key to building and maintaining a successful prayer life. By God's design, having an effective prayer life requires active engagement. In other words, a person's prayer life must be filled with worship, praise, and thanksgiving expressed to our Eternal Father. For example, we begin our prayers by worshiping our Father for who He is and praising Him for His mighty acts. Next, as we continue to worship and praise God, we make our requests known to Him. Before closing prayer, we thank God for being the One who answers prayers.

---

[64] https://digitalbible.ca/article-page/bible-study-symbols-the-tongue-in-the-bible-exploring-its-symbolism-and-significance-1700845119060x3665162486699910300

God Understands You

Receiving answers to prayers does not require eloquent speech. People who are not fluent speakers of their native language can still pray to our Eternal Father and receive answers. Even if an individual has a speech deficiency, that person can use the key ingredients of prayer and receive answers from God. Furthermore, non-verbal individuals can express awe-filled worship, give exuberant praise, and thanksgiving to God. As a result, God will respond to their effectual, fervent prayers.

The Master of communication, who is infinite in wisdom, knowledge, and understanding, is not hindered by linguistic barriers. He is the same God who:

. . . asked Moses, "Who makes a person's mouth? . . . Is it not I, the Lord?"[65]

Therefore, He knows all the codes, symbols, letters, and words that

---

[65] Exodus 4:11- New International Version (NIV).

are used to give meaning to every language. He knows the intricate details of every syntactic rule, every semantic rule, and every contextual rule that governs the use of words.

God knows every version of the braille code. He knows how every assistive listening device works. Furthermore, He clearly understands all the idioms, rhythms, sounds, underlying structures, and vocabulary of every culture. Despite the cultural environment, God clearly understands every emotional overtone, metaphor, and figurative language. He thoroughly understands all verbal as well as non-verbal communication.

The Master of communication understands every word, facial expression, and tone of voice, and He knows the meaning of every cultural body language. While we are trying to conjure up words to articulate our desires, God knows our thoughts before they enter our mind. In fact, He already knows what we need long before we ask. Not only is He thoroughly aware of our needs, but, in eternity, He has already provided all our needs. So, it is left up to us to ask God in faith to manifest on earth what He has already

Following Jesus' Blueprint for Praying Effectual Fervent Prayers provided in eternity.

God Will Answer You

In response to zillions of petitions and intercessions made by people around the world, God knows when and how to answer His people. Without the help of a philologist, God clearly speaks to His people, giving answers that no finite human can provide. God knows how to provide answers on the battlefields of life. So much so, He imparts supernatural strategies that dismantle the schemes of the devil. Amid the battle, God strengthens His dear soldiers to keep lifting "up the protective shield of faith with which [we] can extinguish all the flaming arrows of the evil one."[66]

Even during the cyclones of life, the Master of communication clearly hears our plea for help. During the tempestuous winds of sickness, sorrows, and disappointment, God

---

[66] Ephesians 6:16 - Amplified Bible (AMP).

is ready to rescue us. He specializes in giving peace and deliverance to all who cast their cares upon Him. Just keep on praying because our Father hears us on the day of trouble.[67] If you are in trouble, God is in trouble with you, and He wants you to know – He is bigger than "trouble."

God's Word is true! Certainly, "God is our refuge and strength, a very present help in trouble."[68] At this very moment, whatever you are confronted with, may you find consolation as you use your privilege to

> . . .*pray about everything; tell God your needs, and do not forget to thank Him for His answers. If you do this, you will experience God's peace, which is far more wonderful than the human mind can understand. His peace will keep your thoughts and*

---

[67] Psalm 20:1 - King James Version (KJV).

[68] Psalm 46:1 - King James Version (KJV).

*your [*heart*] quiet and at rest as you trust in Christ*

Jesus.[69]

Be assured, at any time of night or day, our Father is willing, able, and available to answer the prayers of His people.

When God Speaks

Although God is known for answering prayers, He is also known for speaking when no one is petitioning Him for help. Unsolicited help from God serves as a reminder that humans are not always aware of their needs. Also, unsolicited help from God shows His providential care for humans. Due to His unconditional love, God intervenes in the affairs of His people whether they ask for His help or not. Being the Master of communication, God may choose to speak through circumstances, a vision, a dream, an individual, or His written Word.

---

[69] Philippians 4:6-9 - Living Bible (TLB).

Whatever manner God chooses to speak, His voice is powerful and full of majesty.[70] John the Revelator declares, God's voice sounds like "great waters, like the rumbling of mighty thunder, and like the harpists playing on their harps."[71] To me, His voice sounds like music in the air. So, it is important to know, God is not confined to one or two styles of speaking. Hebrews 1:1 declares:

Long ago [our Heavenly Father] spoke in diverse ways to [our earthly fathers] through the prophets, in visions, dreams, and even face to face, telling them little by little about His plans.[72]

Throughout the generations within each dispensation, God used visions and dreams to communicate messages that were relevant to an individual, a group of people, a given phase, or future events.

---

[70] Psalm 29:4 - Amplified Bible (AMP).

[71] Revelation 14:2 - Amplified Bible (AMP).

[72] Hebrews 1:1- Living Bible (TLB).

In addition to speaking through dreams and visions, He is known for communicating through angels,[73] a donkey, [74] and handwriting on the wall.[75] Amazingly, He spoke to Moses through the supernatural manifestation of a burning bush.[76] However, He communicated with Gideon through the manifestation of a wet fleece.[77] On one occasion, He spoke to Samuel in a voice that sounded like Eli.[78]

As strange as it may seem, Jonah received a message from God while he was in the belly of a whale.[79] He spoke to Job out of

---

[73] Luke 1:13-17, Luke 1:30-37, and Luke 2:9-14 – King James Version (KJV).

[74] Numbers 22:21-35 - English Standard Version (ESV).

[75] Daniel 5:5-9 - English Standard Version (ESV).

[76] Exodus 3 – King James Version (KJV).

[77] Judges 6 - King James Version (KJV).

[78] 1 Samuel 3 - King James Version (KJV).

[79] Jonah 1-4 - King James Version (KJV).

the storm.[80] But there are times when God speaks in a low whisper.[81] God is also known for communicating His plan and purposes through the simplicity of sermonizing. In one setting, the Master of communication uses one profound message and breaks it up like bread to feed the multitude.

The Master of communication articulates His eternal thoughts through the mouth of the preacher. God also speaks out of His written word as we prayerfully study the Scriptures. Through the inspired Word of God, we receive lessons for life. 2 Timothy 3:16-17 declares:

There is nothing like the written Word of God for showing you the way to salvation through faith in Christ Jesus. Every part of Scripture is God-breathed and useful one way or another - showing us

---

[80] Job 38:1 - New International Version (NIV).

[81] 1 Kings 19:11-13 - English Standard Version (ESV).

truth, exposing our rebellion, correcting our

mistakes, training us to live God's way. Through the

Word we are put together and shaped up for the tasks

God has for us.[82]

Whatever the task may be, we must trust and acknowledge the Lord in everything we do. Furthermore, during the entire process of completing the God-ordained tasks, we must pray without ceasing.

---

[82] 2 Timothy 3:16-17 – The Message Bible (MSG).

Chapter 6
Praying Constantly

God created humans to commune with Him through a direct line of communication. Sadly, through the rebellious and sinful act of Adam and Eve, the direct line of communication was broken. Nevertheless, through the atoning sacrifice of Christ, Spirit-filled believers have been reconciled to God. Now, we are citizens of God's Kingdom. As a result, we have the authority, privilege, and responsibility to pray effectual fervent prayers.

> *The effectual fervent prayer is a powerful, God-given pathway into the miraculous power of God. Through this pathway, God's eternal purpose is transferred from the heavenly realm to the earthly realm.*[83]

Thank God for giving us the pathway of prayer, where we can

---

[83] A definition for prayer given to Dr. Gwen E. Brannum from our Heavenly Father after she was born of the water and of the Spirit in 1984.

Following Jesus' Blueprint for Praying Effectual Fervent Prayers

communicate with Him any time of night or day.

Based on the teachings of Jesus, we should always pray and never quit. Praying constantly is an essential element of victorious living. On the surface, the thought of constantly praying might appear to be impossible. However, careful observation of God's infallible Word reveals the principles to follow to fulfill the mandate to constantly pray. On one occasion,

> *Jesus told His disciples a story showing that it was necessary for them to pray consistently and never quit. . .*[84]

Jesus' statement correlates with the Apostle Paul's directive for Spirit-filled believers to "pray without ceasing."[85]

Praying constantly is far more than bending your knees, closing your eyes, bowing your head, and saying words aloud. To

---

[84] Luke 18:1 - Living Bible (TLB).

[85] 1 Thessalonians 5:17 – King James Version (KJV).

actively engage in constant prayer simply means we must be mindful of God in everything we do, acknowledge Him in all our ways, and thank Him as He directs our paths. With that thought in mind, trusting God, and acknowledging Him in all our ways requires constant interaction with Him throughout the day. To interact or collaborate with God to fulfill His plan and purposes, there must be an open line of communication. In other words, we must constantly be in the mode of prayer, listening for the voice of God.

Another aspect of being constantly prayerful includes being attuned to the voice of God and responding appropriately whenever He speaks. Often, the answers that we have sought God for on our knees show up while we are on our feet—busy and about our Father's business. God is in the business of speaking, revealing His glory, and giving insight while we are conducting our daily affairs. In fact, He is known for speaking through the happenings of the day.

When our Father speaks, we should respond right there on the spot with a "thank You, Lord, I will obey Your voice," or simply acknowledge Him in your own unique way—that is a brief prayer.

Or God might give you an answer during a board meeting at work. Right there on the spot, if you "quietly" acknowledge His presence and thank Him for His answer—that is a brief prayer. Lengthy or brief, God hears our prayers whenever and wherever we seek to commune with Him.

Pray Everywhere

Contrary to the idea that praying must be restricted to being in church, at a shrine, or at a pagoda, we are to pray everywhere. "Everywhere" means wherever we are at any given time of the day. God wants to communicate with us constantly throughout the day, wherever we are. Based on the teachings of Jesus, being constant in prayer is a divine strategy for experiencing victory over the frailties of the flesh, trials, and temptations. Through prayer, our discernment is sharpened, and we learn how to recognize the tactics of the devil and combat the forces of darkness.

Since the forces of darkness exist throughout the world, we

must stay alert, so we can resist the devil while standing strong in the Lord. Staying alert requires constant prayer. 1 Peter 5:8-9 highlights the necessity of praying constantly by saying:

Be sober, well balanced, and self-disciplined, [always be alert and cautious]. That enemy of yours, the devil, prowls around like a roaring lion fiercely hungry, seeking someone to devour. But resist him, be firm in your faith against his attack—rooted, established, immovable, knowing that the same experiences of suffering are being experienced by your "brothers and sisters" throughout the world. You do not suffer alone.[86]

To remain sober and vigilant, we must constantly pray and seek guidance from God. In addition to praying for ourselves, we must also pray for our "brothers and sisters" all over the world.

---

[86] 1 Peter 5:8-9 - Amplified Bible (AMP).

Prayers are needed every day, all day, and everywhere. Therefore, we should pray always and never quit. Not only should we pray in secret, on the mountain, or in the valley, but we should also pray everywhere. Through constant prayer, we gain the necessary strength to properly behave as we encounter internal as well as external conflict.

Triumph Over Conflict

All humans will encounter either internal or external conflict. Internal conflicts include struggles about religious beliefs, ethics, relationships, work, and societal systems. External conflicts include struggles against another individual, natural forces, technological issues, and societal norms. Whether internal or external, we can triumph over conflict through prayer. For example, if we encounter the internal struggle of religious conflict, we can gain strength through prayer. God will strengthen us to practice equanimity and intuitive intelligence, which will produce resolutions that will glorify Him.

God is known for revealing His glory during societal conflicts. Unlike internal conflicts, societal conflicts involve external factors that challenge an individual's ethics, morals, and values. One of the major concerns relevant to societal conflicts is dealing with the struggle of balancing self-needs with societal expectations. With that thought in mind, it is essential to seek guidance from God as we endeavor to promote psychospiritual well-being and social cohesion. Remember, our all-knowing Father knows the intricate details of the psychology behind internal and societal conflicts. He knows the origination of humans' struggles.

Internal conflict and external conflict became evident in the Garden of Eden. Adam and Eve experienced external conflict with God due to their disobedience to His command when they ate from the forbidden tree. Then, they experienced internal conflict, feeling guilt and shame after recognizing their transgression. Worst of all, their internal conflict intensified as they experienced being alienated from God. Nevertheless, God revealed His glory through an expression of His providential care and unconditional love.

God continued to reveal His glory everywhere humans fell prey to internal and external conflicts. For example, God's glory was revealed in the life of Moses. Although God chose Moses to be a prophet, lawgiver, and leader, he experienced internal and external conflicts. While Moses was caught in the middle of his struggles,

> *he went to see his own people and watched them suffering under forced labor. He saw a Hebrew, one of his own people, being beaten by an Egyptian. He looked all around, and when he did not see anyone, he beat the Egyptian to death and hid the body in the sand.*[87]

As the story unfolds, Moses was made aware there were others who knew about his attempt to cover up his actions. As a result, he left Egypt and went to Midian.

God revealed His glory in Midian by connecting Moses to a

---

[87] Exodus 2:11-15 - GOD'S WORD Translation (GW).

priest named Jethro, who was also a shepherd. While working with Jethro, Moses had an opportunity to reflect on the teachings he received from his mother. For the first twelve years of Moses' life, his mother taught him about the boundless God of the universe. Then, until he was approximately forty years old, Pharaoh taught Moses how to oversee the affairs of Egypt. But God had bigger plans for Moses.

Before the foundation of the world, God chose Moses to be a type of Christ. Despite the internal and external conflict Moses experienced, he was destined to be a lawgiver, prophet, deliverer, and shepherd. By God's design, Moses would have forty years to commune with God in prayer as He prepared him for the task ahead. God knew the intricate details of Moses' struggles, but He still desired to reveal His glory in Moses' life. He still loved communing with Moses in prayer.

After communing with God for forty years, something wonderful happened between God and Moses. One day,

Moses was keeping the flock of Jethro (Reuel) his

father-in-law, the priest of Midian; and he led his flock to the west side of the wilderness and came to Horeb (Sinai), the mountain of God. The Angel of the Lord appeared to him in a blazing flame of fire from the midst of a bush; and he looked, and behold, the bush was on fire, yet it was not consumed. So, Moses said, "I must turn away [from the flock] and see this great sight—why the bush is not burned up." When the Lord saw that he turned away [from the flock] to look, God called to him from the midst of the bush and said, "Moses, Moses!" And he said, "Here I am." [88]

Saying, "Here I am," was a sure sign that Moses was attuned to the voice of God.

While God was speaking, He addressed Moses' internal and

---

[88] Exodus 3:1-4 - Amplified Bible (AMP).

external conflicts. Watch the process,

> *The Lord said, "I have in fact seen the affliction*
> *(suffering, desolation) of My people who are in*
> *Egypt, and have heard their cry because of their*
> *taskmasters (oppressors); for I know their pain and*
> *suffering. So, I have come down to rescue them from*
> *the hand (power) of the Egyptians, and to bring them*
> *up from that land to a land [that is] good and*
> *spacious, to a land flowing with milk and honey [a*
> *land of plenty]—to the place of the Canaanite, the*
> *Hittite, the Amorite, the Perizzite, the Hivite, and the*
> *Jebusite.*[89]

Just imagine the striking contrast between the bondage that was being experienced in Egypt and the freedom that exist in Canaan. Moses must have felt extraordinary joy hearing how God was going

---

[89] Exodus 3:7-9 - Amplified Bible (AMP).

Following Jesus' Blueprint for Praying Effectual Fervent Prayers

to deliver the Israelites out of bondage.

As God continued to speak, He revealed His plan concerning

the deliverance of His people. Speaking directly to Moses, God said,

> *come now, and I will send you to Pharaoh, and then*
>
> *bring My people, the children of Israel, out of*
>
> *Egypt." But Moses said to God, "Who am I, that I*
>
> *should go to Pharaoh, and that I should bring the*
>
> *children of Israel out of Egypt?" And God said,*
>
> *"Certainly I will be with you, and this shall be the*
>
> *sign to you that it is I who have sent you: when you*
>
> *have brought the people out of Egypt, you shall serve*
>
> *and worship God at this mountain."[90]*

Notice how Moses struggled with his internal conflicts concerning

his identity and his insecurities. The struggle was so great he asked

God, "Who am I, that I should go to Pharaoh, and that I should bring

---

[90] Exodus 3:10-12 - Amplified Bible (AMP).

the children of Israel out of Egypt?"[91]

Without rebuking Moses for His lack of confidence, God compassionately answered Moses by saying, "Certainly I will be with you . . ." Those same words are ringing out of eternity in the life of every believer. In the days ahead, whatever internal or external conflicts we encounter, God will be with us. In fact, He is with us right now, and He will never leave us. Since God is with us, we can ask Him for guidance as we encounter internal or external conflicts. In response to our prayers, God will impart divine strategies for addressing conflict that will foster strength and balance.

Now, consider how God strengthened Elijah and provided balance for him as he encountered conflicts. The Bible reveals Elijah experienced external conflict through Ahab and Jezebel. At the same time, he experienced internal conflicts that manifested in the form

---

[91] Exodus 3:11 - Amplified Bible (AMP).

Following Jesus' Blueprint for Praying Effectual Fervent Prayers

of fear, moments of doubt, disillusion, and depression. Nevertheless,

he was a man of prayer. So much so, James 5:17 states:

> *Elijah was a human being, even as we are. He prayed*
>
> *earnestly that it would not rain, and it did not rain*
>
> *on the land for three and a half years. Again, he*
>
> *prayed, and the heavens gave rain, and the earth*
>
> *produced its crops.*[92]

Despite Elijah's internal and external conflicts, he constantly

prayed, and the glory of God was revealed. As a result, lives were

transformed.

Elijah and Moses are extraordinary examples of how to

triumph over internal and external conflicts through constant prayer.

However, our greatest example is Jesus, because He "was in all

points tempted like as we are, yet without sin."[93] While our sinless

---

[92] James 5:17-18 - New International Version (NIV).

[93] Hebrews 4:15b - King James Version (KJV).

example hung on the cross, He was tempted once again to prove His deity. Just as He triumphed over the temptations of the wilderness, He triumphed over the internal and external conflict He experienced on the cross. He had successfully triumphed over conflict before, and He did it again.

While triumphing over external conflict on the cross, Jesus prayed, "Father, forgive them; for they know not what they do."[94] As He triumphed over internal conflict, He cried with a loud voice and prayed, saying, "Father, into thy hands I commend my spirit: and having said thus, he gave up the ghost."[95] Jesus Christ, our Lord and Savior, showed us how to prayerfully triumph over conflict as well as how to complete our mission on earth. Leaving no room for doubt, this same Jesus who said ". . . be of good cheer, I have overcome the world" is the same One who cried aloud, "It is

---

[94] Luke 23:34 - King James Version (KJV).

[95] Luke 23:46 - King James Version (KJV).

finished!"

After Jesus finished His redemptive work on the cross, He entered the heavens as our High Priest. He did not go with the blood of bulls and goats to make atonement for our sins, but with His own precious blood, He purchased our forgiveness. By His crucifixion, Jesus became the ultimate lamb of sacrifice and did away with the animal sacrifices. Hallelujah! All because of our Great High Priest, we do not have to slay lambs anymore.

Jesus freely gave Himself "like a lamb that is led to the slaughter."[96] The Savior of the world was "wounded for our transgressions, He was crushed for our wickedness—our sin, our injustice, our wrongdoing. The punishment required for our well-being fell on Him."[97] 1 John 2:2 emphatically states: "He is the propitiation for our sins: and not for ours only, but also for the sins

---

[96] Isaiah 53:7 - Amplified Bible (AMP).

[97] Isaiah 53:5 - Amplified Bible (AMP).

of the whole world."[98]

Before He laid down His life for us, Jesus interceded for His disciples and future believers. Now that He has finished the work of redemption, He is standing on our behalf, making intercession for us continually.

> *Seeing then that we have a Great High Priest, who is passed into the heavens, Jesus the Son of God, let us hold fast our profession. Let us therefore come boldly to the throne of grace, that we may obtain mercy, and find grace to help in time of need.*[99]

Jesus paved the pathway of prayer that leads directly to the throne of God. Therefore, He is the Master Teacher of praying effectual fervent prayers.

---

[98] 1 John 2:2 - King James Version (KJV).

[99] Hebrews 4:14 & 16 - King James Version (KJV).

Chapter 7

The Master Teacher

From a natural perspective, an expert teacher gives students a profound understanding of a given subject and helps to establish a solid foundation for future learning. Additionally, the expert teacher invests time in getting to know the student and provides tailored instructions that coincide with the student's personal needs. Furthermore, the expert teacher provides a supportive learning environment and various tools needed for the development of critical thinking skills. The expert teacher's goal is to assist students in reaching their fullest potential.

Although there are diverse types of expert teachers, there is only one infinite Master Teacher, and His name is Jesus. His teachings are so profound that all other learnings are without enduring value unless they are built upon the instructions He provides. His instructions lay a solid foundation for future learning and offer clear steps for turning away from ungodliness and worldly desires. As the "way, truth, and life," Jesus provides an unmistakable path to reconciliation with God.

Indeed, this Master Teacher is the sole means of receiving eternal life. Even the words He speak are "spirit, and they are life."[100] Therefore, it is wise to obey His teachings. In fact, Jesus said:

> . . .whosoever heareth these sayings of mine, and doeth them, I will liken him unto a wise man. . . everyone that heareth these sayings of mine, and doeth them not, shall be likened unto a foolish man. . . the people were astonished at His doctrine: For He taught them as one having authority, and not as the scribes.[101]

Although the scribes were highly educated and renowned as expert

---

[100] John 6:63b - King James Version (KJV).

[101] Matthew 7:24-29 - King James Version (KJV).

teachers of Jewish law and tradition, they still had much to learn from the infinite Master Teacher.

There is an old proverb that states, "If the student has not learned, the teacher has not taught." However, this is not always true. Many people heard Jesus' teachings but failed to learn from them. As seen in John 6:66-67, people turned away from the Master Teacher, refusing to accept His guidance. Nevertheless, Jesus continued providing tailored instructions that coincided with the needs of His followers. While addressing the universal needs of humanity, He used examples, parables, and sermons to impart profound principles about prayer.

When You Pray

In His famous discourse, "The Sermon on the Mount," Jesus said, "When you pray," emphasizing the necessity of prayer. Prayer is of supreme importance, and it affects every aspect of life. To guide us through the process of reaping the benefits of prayer,

Jesus revealed His blueprint and principles for praying effectual, fervent prayers. His entire ministry focused on reconciling humans to God, equipping them to be effective citizens of God's Kingdom, and teaching them how to be constant in prayer.

Before Jesus started His public ministry of teaching, healing, and meeting the needs of the people, He exemplified the importance of prayer. Luke 3:21-22 states:

> *When all the people were being baptized, Jesus was baptized too. And as He was praying, heaven was opened, and the Holy Spirit descended on Him in bodily form like a dove.*[102]

The first record of Jesus praying, the entire atmosphere shifted, and the glory of God was revealed.[103]

Matthew 4:1-4 recounts how, after His baptism, the Holy

---

[102] Luke 3:21-22 - New International Version (NIV).

[103] Matthew 3:13-17, Mark 1:9-11, and Luke 3:21-23.

Following Jesus' Blueprint for Praying Effectual Fervent Prayers

Spirit led Jesus into the wilderness to be tempted by the devil.

> *And the tempter came and said to Him, "If You are*
> *the Son of God, command that these stones become*
> *bread." But Jesus replied, "It is written and forever*
> *remains written, 'Man shall not live by bread alone,*
> *but by every word that comes out of the mouth of*
> *God.*[104]

Through prayer, Jesus triumphed over temptations. In fact, He demonstrated how fasting and praying position us to receive divine strategies for combating the forces of darkness. Although there is a drastic difference between the scene at Jesus' baptism and the scene of Him being in the wilderness, in both cases, He prayed, and the glory of God was revealed.

Every aspect of Jesus' prayer life demonstrated the principles He taught concerning effectual, fervent prayers. After

---

[104] Matthew 4:1-4 - Amplified Bible (AMP).

Jesus started His public ministry, He continued a life of prayer. Luke 6:12-13 says:

> *One day [Jesus] went out into the mountains to pray and prayed all night. At daybreak He called together His followers and chose twelve of them to be the inner circle of His disciples . . .*[105]

Next, the Master Teacher showed His disciples that prayer is more important than our social life.

Of course, Jesus knows the importance of social interactions. He knows how social connections provide a sense of belonging, emotional support, and how they assist with maintaining mental and physical health. However, Jesus exemplified the supreme importance of communing with God in solitude. After feeding a multitude of people,

> *. . . Jesus made the disciples get into the boat and go*

---

[105] Luke 6:12-13 - Living Bible (TLB).

on ahead of Him to the other side, while He

dismissed the crowd. After He had dismissed them,

He went up on a mountainside by Himself to pray.

Later that night, He was there alone. . .[106]

Following Jesus' example, we must take the initiative to dismiss the crowd. Dismissing the crowd includes turning off the phone, notifications, and alarms. Additionally, dismissing the crowd means abstaining from responding to texts and emails.

Learning from the examples of Jesus, it is important to pray in solitude during various times of the day. In Matthew 14:22-23, Jesus was alone in the evening. On the other hand, Mark 1:35 reveals,

Early in the morning, while it was still dark, Jesus

got up, left the house, and went off to a solitary place,

---

[106] Matthew 14:22-23 - New International Version (NIV).

where He prayed.[107]

On another occasion, Jesus showed us the necessity of praying all night. As the Master Teacher, it was necessary for Jesus to demonstrate the importance of praying during each prayer watch.

The Master Teacher also revealed the value of praying in public. While standing at Lazarus' tomb, Jesus prayed in front of the crowd for a specific reason. Watch the process,

Jesus lifted His eyes and said, "Father, I thank you that you have heard me. I knew that you always hear me, but I said this on account of the people standing around, that they may believe that you sent me." When He had said these things, He cried out with a loud voice, "Lazarus, come out." The man who had died came out, his hands and feet bound with linen strips, and his face wrapped with a cloth. Jesus said

---

[107] Mark 1:35 - New International Version (NIV).

to them, "Unbind him, and let him go." Many of the

Jews therefore, who had come with Mary and had

seen what He did, believed in Him. . .[108]

There are times when praying in public gives others an opportunity to see and hear the protocol for praying an effectual fervent prayer. Additionally, praying publicly gives way to others seeing a demonstration of God's glory being revealed in the form of a miracle. All of which can lead to people believing in God.

Understanding our assignment and being sensitive to the move of God is key to how we should conduct ourselves during public prayer. In addition to exemplifying the importance of public prayer, Jesus showed His disciples how to pray—prayers of thanksgiving[109] as well as brief prayers.[110] Jesus' prayer life had a significant impact on His disciples. So much so,

---

[108] John 11:41-45 - English Standard Version (ESV).

[109] Matthew 15:36 and Matthew 11:25-26 - King James Version (KJV).

[110] John 12:27-38 - King James Version (KJV).

One day Jesus was praying in a certain place. When

he finished, one of his disciples said to Him, "Lord,

teach us to pray, just as John taught his disciples."[111]

In response to the disciples' request, Jesus revealed the blueprint for praying effectual prayers, also known as "The Lord's Prayer."

---

[111] Luke 11:1 - New International Version (NIV).

Chapter 8

Jesus' Blueprint for Praying

Jesus is the Master teacher of praying effectual, fervent prayers. Not only did He teach about prayer using parables and illustrations, but He also exemplified the discipline of prayer from the start until the end of His earthly ministry. He is seen praying during His baptism as well as on the cross. Through prayer, Jesus triumphed over the lust of the flesh, the lust of the eyes, and the pride of life. In fact, *He was tempted in all points like as we are, yet without sin.*[112]

Being the greatest Prayer Warrior that ever prayed, Jesus knows how to navigate the pathway of prayer. He understands the intricate details of how to approach the very throne of God. In fact, through His atoning sacrifice, Jesus bridged the gap between God and humans, making it possible for us to have direct access to God through spiritual adoption. The very moment an individual is adopted into God's family, that person has the privilege to call the infinite God of the universe—Father.

---

[112] Hebrews 4:15 – Kings James Version (KJV).

95

Abba Father in Heaven

In the Garden of Gethsemane, Jesus prayed, "Abba Father, all things are possible for You. Take this cup away from Me; nevertheless, not what I will, but what You will."[113] Certainly, it was God's will for Jesus to be *the propitiation for our sins, and not for ours only, but for the sins of the entire world*."[114] Fulfilling the will of the Father, Jesus finished the work of redemption. At that very moment, He tore down the middle wall of partition,[115] making it possible for us to boldly approach the ". . . throne of God and stay there to receive His mercy and to find grace to help us in our times of need"[116]

To experience the reality of having direct access to the throne of God, an individual must repent, turn to the One who is able to forgive sin, be born of the water, and be born of the Spirit. Then, that person becomes a child of God through a spiritual adoption. Just think, through the atoning sacrifice of Jesus, we are made the children of God. No wonder the writer of 1 John 2:2 wrote:

---

[113] Mark 14:36 - King James Version (KJV).

[114] 1 John 2:2 - King James Version (KJV).

[115] Ephesians 2:14-18 - King James Version (KJV).

[116] Hebrews 4:16 - Living Bible (TLB).

See what an incredible quality of love the Father has shown to us, that we would [be permitted to] be named and called and counted the children of God! And so, we are![117]

Now that we are God's children, we have the privilege to call Him "Abba Father."

When we pray saying, "Abba Father," we are, in fact, addressing the infinite source of all existence. Our Father owns the "earth and the fulness thereof, the world and they that dwell therein."[118] He is King of kings and Lord of lords. He is "Wonderful, Counsellor, the Mighty God, and the Everlasting Father."[119] Hallelujah! The Almighty God is our Father, and we have the privilege to commune with Him in prayer.

With awe-filled worship, we can approach the very throne of God. In humble adoration, we worship our High and Holy Father for being omniscient, omnipresent, and omnipotent. Also, we reverence Him for being infinite, immutable, and self-sufficient. Furthermore, we exalt Him for being faithful, just, gracious, and merciful. The

---

[117] 1 John 3:1 – Amplified Bible (AMP).

[118] Psalms 24:1 - King James Version (KJV).

[119] Isaiah 9:6 - King James Version (KJV).

more we worship God for who He is, the more of Himself He reveals to us on a personal level. As a result, we gain greater appreciation for our Heavenly Father.

With hearts filled with adoration, we joyfully pray, "Our Father who art in Heaven." At this point, we are honoring our Father for being the God of the universe who transcends all space and time. With awe-filled worship, we honor Him for being the Supreme Ruler who has preeminence over all His creation. Bowing in humble adoration, we worship Our Father for being the only High and Holy One who condescends to our low estate. Amazingly, our Father, in whom we live and have our being[120]—lives in the hearts of His Children.

Furthermore, when we address God as being the One who is in heaven, we are acknowledging His place of authority. We are boasting over the fact that our "God [our Father] is in heaven; He does whatever pleases Him."[121] Glory hallelujah! The boundless God of the universe chose us to be His very own before the foundation of the world. What He declared in eternity has been manifested in time. Now, through the atoning sacrifice of Jesus, we

---

[120] Acts 17:28 - Amplified Bible (AMP).

[121] Psalm 115:3 - New International Version (NIV).

are the children of God who have the privilege to represent our Father's name.

May Your Holy Name Be Honored

God's name has always been, still is, and will forever be "majestic and glorious and excellent in all the earth!"[122] His name is holy. In other words, God's name is sacred, above all other names, and should be reverence. Furthermore, God's name is intrinsically linked to His sovereignty.

Recognizing the divine sovereignty of God, Jacob, Moses, Manoah, and others wanted to know His name. But the name of our Father remained a mystery for years, making it impossible for the Old Testament saints to relate to God in the same manner as the New Testament saints. With the revelation of the name of Jesus, we have the privilege to build an intimate relationship with our Heavenly Father.

One of the greatest gifts our Father bestowed upon His children is His name. With the privilege of bearing the name of our Father comes the responsibility to represent His name in grand style.

---

[122] Psalms 8:9 - Amplified Bible (AMP).

As children of God, we are:

> *. . . a chosen race, a royal priesthood, a consecrated nation, a [special] people for God's own possession, so that [we] may proclaim the excellencies [the wonderful deeds and virtues and perfections] of Him who called [us] out of darkness into His marvelous light.*[123]

Therefore, we must pray for wisdom to behave in a manner compatible with our status as children of God. We must constantly pray, worshipping God for who He is and praising Him for His mighty acts, so we will remain mindful that our Father's name is attached to His character and reputation. Although we can do nothing to enhance the holiness of God's name, we can certainly honor and bring glory to His name by living a life of sanctification.

Honoring our Father's name is more than words; it is a lifestyle. The Bible reveals ways to honor and bring glory to the name of our Father. First, we must fear God [worship Him with awe-filled reverence, knowing that He is Almighty God] and keep His commandments.[124] Another way to bring glory to our Father's name

---

[123] 1 Peter 2:9 - Amplified Bible (AMP).

[124] Ecclesiastes 12:13 - Amplified Bible (AMP).

is to exude the "Fruit of the Spirit" in every area of our lives. Galatians 5:22-23 states:

> *The fruit of the Spirit [the result of His presence within us] is love [unselfish concern for others], joy, [inner] peace, patience [not the ability to wait, but how we act while waiting], kindness, goodness, faithfulness, gentleness, self-control. Against such things there is no law.*[125]

Certainly, it is my prayer that our Father's name continues to be highly esteemed by His dear children throughout the world. Also, I am persistently praying for the advancement of God's Kingdom.

May Your Kingdom Come

From a natural perspective, every Kingdom throughout the world has a king or queen who oversees its affairs. However, all rulers and kingdoms of this world will eventually pass away. But the Kingdom of God and its eternal King will exist forever. All kingdoms also have a specific domain, royal covenants, governing principles, an army, a code of ethics, commonwealth, and a social

---

[125] Galatians 5:22-23 - Amplified Bible (AMP).

culture. However, God's Kingdom is not limited to mankind's imperfect view of earthly institutions or affiliations, whether they are religious or secular.

The Kingdom of God transcends the boundaries of earthly realms, encompassing the entire earth. Although citizens of God's Kingdom are spread across various nations, their principal loyalty must be to the King of kings and His eternal Kingdom. While Kingdom citizens may express profound patriotism towards their earthly nations, their foremost dedication should invariably be to God's sovereign rule. Therefore, it is imperative that Kingdom citizens consistently "seek first the Kingdom of God and His righteousness." Moreover, they should earnestly strive to advance God's Kingdom through prayer, remaining mindful of its past, present, and future significance.

God's Kingdom will reach its full realization upon the return of Jesus in the future. However, the Kingdom of God is presently accessible through the atoning sacrifice of Jesus Christ. In this current era, the Kingdom of God is manifested in the hearts of Spirit-filled believers. Consequently, we, as citizens of God's Kingdom, possess the authority and privilege to offer effectual, fervent prayers that will impact the lives of individuals globally. Therefore, it is imperative that we pray for the establishment of God's Kingdom in the hearts of people across various spheres of the marketplace, within our families and neighborhoods, and among individuals worldwide.

Remember, our prayers can be lengthy or brief. In fact, our prayer can be as simple as this:

> Heavenly Father, we adore You for being the Only wise God, our Savior. You have preeminence over everything. We honor Your presence. Thank You for giving us an opportunity to be placed in Your Kingdom. Now, draw us closer to You so we can represent Your Kingdom and Your name in royal style. Strengthen, energized, and fortify us as we continue to "seek first the Kingdom of God and Your righteousness." Shield and protect the citizens of Your Kingdom as we share the Gospel of Jesus Christ. Transform the lives of our loved ones, co-workers, neighbors, friends, and people throughout the world. Be glorified in the lives of Your people. In the Mighty Name of Jesus, we pray. Amen!

May Your Will Be Done

On His way to the cross, Jesus completed His earthly ministry to the multitude, His training of the disciples, His Last Supper with them, His High Priestly Prayer, and His final sermon.

Then, He faced arrest, cruelty, indescribable pain, an illegal trial, and death by crucifixion. To maneuver through the agony of His indescribable spiritual conflict, Jesus chose a place to pray just outside Jerusalem called Gethsemane. As Jesus prayed, He experienced a struggle that our finite minds will never fully comprehend.

Jesus' struggle was not over whether He would redeem humans from sin, but over how that redemption would occur. Although the intricate details of Jesus' struggle remain a mystery, we do know the struggle was so excruciating that:

> [Jesus] *fell face downward on the ground and prayed, 'My Father! If it is possible, let this cup be taken away from me. But I want your will, not mine.* '[126]

Jesus' struggle was between the divine will and the human will.

While all of God's wrath regarding the destructive power of sin was aimed at Jesus' perfect sacrifice, He was crushed beyond measure. Luke the physician explained:

> *Being in agony, deeply distressed and anguished; 'almost' to the point of death,* [Jesus] *prayed more*

---

[126] Matthew 26:39 - Living Bible (TLB).

intently; and His sweat became like drops of blood,
falling on the ground.[127]

Despite the agony Jesus experienced, He was persistent in prayer. Notice, His second prayer was different from His first. He prayed in Matthew 26:42, "My Father, if this cannot pass away unless I drink it, Your will be done."[128] Submitting to the will of God, Jesus accepted the drinking of the bitter cup and yielded Himself to the task at hand. Through prayer, Jesus fought and won another spiritual battle in the Garden of Gethsemane. Once again, Jesus triumphed over internal and external conflict.

On His way to the cross, Jesus demonstrated the doctrine of obedience by submitting to the will of God. Additionally, by His willingness to leave the garden as the captive of the guards, Jesus demonstrated His boundless love for humanity. Furthermore, careful observation of Jesus' time of testing reveals three significant principles about the seasons of testing: 1) they are permitted by God, 2) they are proportioned by God, and 3) God has a purpose for our times of testing.

Learning from Jesus' example, we must be persistent in

---

[127] Luke 22:44 - Amplified Bible (AMP).

[128] Matthew 26:42 - Amplified Bible (AMP).

prayer as we go through our times of testing. Additionally, we must remember that the only way to achieve victory in a spiritual fight is to use spiritual weapons. The spiritual weapons of faith, truth, righteousness, salvation, the gospel, and the word of God fortify us when they are effectively used in the atmosphere of prayer. While using our spiritual weapons, we must pray "Heavenly Father, not my will but let your will be done."

Give Us the Bread We Need Today

Following Jesus' pattern and principles for praying sets the stage for us to ask God to supply even the smallest of our needs. Watch the process. First, we highly esteem our Father for who He is, we worship Him for having preeminence over all, we adore Him for being the infinite God of the universe, and we praise Him for His mighty acts. As we worship God in *spirit and in truth*,[129] He increases our desire to be loyal citizens of His Kingdom. As a result, our deepest desire is to please our King. So, prior to petitioning God to supply personal needs, we "seek first the Kingdom of God and His righteousness."[130]

---

[129] John 4.24 - King James Version (KJV).

[130] Matthew 6:33a - English Standard Version (ESV).

When we genuinely seek God, we bask in His presence and listen for His voice. This is a good place to actively practice Psalm 37:4 in the atmosphere of prayer. So, during prayer, we bask in God's presence, we delight ourselves in the Lord, and [our Father] gives us the desires *and* petitions of our hearts."[131] In other words, God gives us a spiritual alignment by allowing His thoughts to transform our thoughts, speech, and actions. During the process, He releases greater insight concerning His plan and purpose for our lives.

Having greater understanding of what God desires, all we must do is "Commit everything [we] do to the Lord. Trust Him, and He will help [us]."[132] He will help us to be busy and about our Father's business. In the meanwhile, He will remind us not to "grow weary while doing good, for in due season we shall reap if we do not lose heart."[133] With that thought in mind, we are confident that God will supply all our needs both spiritually and naturally.

Prior to telling His disciples, "seek first the Kingdom of God

---

[131] Psalm 37:4 - Amplified Bible (AMP).

[132] Psalm 37:5 - New Living Translation (NLT).

[133] Galatians 6:9 - New King James Version (NKJV).

and His righteousness,"[134] Jesus reminded His disciples that our Heavenly Father is thoroughly aware of our needs. In fact, He said:

> *do not be anxious, saying, 'What shall we eat?' or 'What shall we drink?' or 'What shall we wear?' For the Gentiles seek after all these things, and your heavenly Father knows that you need them all.*[135]

Although God knows all our needs and has *given us all things which pertain unto life and godliness,*[136] as dear children, we must always exude respect and simply ask Him to give us our daily bread.

Remember, if we ask for bread, our Father will never give us a stone. Jesus said:

> *If you, then, though you are evil, know how to give good gifts to your children, how much more will your Father in heaven give good gifts to those who ask Him!*[137]

As dear children, "This is the confidence we have in approaching

---

[134] Matthew 6:33a - English Standard Version (ESV).

[135] Matthew 6:31-32 - English Standard Version (ESV).

[136] 2 Peter 1:3 - King James Version (KJV).

[137] Matthew 7:11 - New International Version (NIV).

[our Father]: that if we ask anything according to His will, He hears us."[138] Whether we are asking for natural or spiritual bread, God hears us!

Forgive Us as We Forgive Others

Divine forgiveness is deeply embedded in the story of humanity. The need for forgiveness started with Adam and Eve when they disobeyed God and ate from the forbidden tree. Their disobedience resulted in death from two perspectives: 1) they immediately died spiritually, which disengaged their intimate relationship with God; and 2) They began the process of aging that eventually culminated in their physical death. But God, who is rich in mercy, allowed Adam to live 930 years before he died physically. God's mercy is the principle upon which the doctrine of forgiveness is built.

In His loving kindness, God has made provision for sinners to be relieved from the penalty of their transgressions through forgiveness. In the case of Adam and Eve, instead of immediately cutting them off, God provided them with clothing, granted them more years of life, and gave them a promise that one of their

---

[138] 1 John 5:14 - Amplified Bible (AMP).

offspring would take vengeance upon the adversary of their souls. Leading up to the fulfillment of His promise, God provided a working solution through the sacrifices of animals. For almost two thousand years, from Moses to Christ, the blood of animal sacrifices brought divine pardon and forgiveness for sin. The animal sacrifices were symbolic of the redemptive death of Christ on the cross.

At the appointed time, the Lamb of God came in the likeness of sinful flesh to take the place of the sacrificial lambs. Announcing His arrival, John the Baptist said, "Look! The Lamb of God who takes away the sin of the world!"[139] Before Jesus offered Himself as the ultimate and final sacrifice for sins, He taught about the necessity of forgiving and being forgiven. He also taught that those who refuse to show mercy to others disqualify themselves from receiving the mercy and forgiveness of God. Jesus knows the intricate details of humans' propensity to seek revenge for wrongs committed against them. However, He wants us to follow a more charitable way by loving and forgiving others.

Based on the teachings of Jesus, forgiveness is not a once-in-a-lifetime event. In fact, we must practice forgiveness daily. Notice, The Lord's prayer teaches us to say:

---

[139] John 1:29 – Amplified Bible (AMP).

Give us this day our daily bread. And forgive us our debts, as we have forgiven our debtors [letting go of both the wrong and the resentment]. [140]

Unforgiveness has a detrimental impact on our relationship with God. Mathew 6:15 puts if like this:

. . .if you do not forgive others [nurturing your hurt and anger with the result that it interferes with your relationship with God], then your Father will not forgive your trespasses. [141]

Without exceptions, forgiveness is necessary, and by God's design, forgiveness is liberating. The good news is "if [we] forgive others their trespasses—their reckless and willful sins, [our] Heavenly Father will also forgive [us]." [142]

Keep Us Safe for Your Glory

At the Last Supper, Jesus prayed for Himself, His followers, and future believers. While praying for His disciples, He said:

---

[140] Matthew 6:11-12 – Amplified Bible (AMP).

[141] Matthew 6:15 – Amplified Bible (AMP).

[142] Matthew 6:14 – Amplified Bible (AMP).

I do not ask You to take them out of the world, but that You keep them and protect them from the evil one.[143]

Jesus desired for His followers to be kept safe, sanctified, and made holy by the truth of God's Word. As He shifted from praying for His disciples to praying for future believers He said:

I do not pray for these alone [it is not for their sake only that I make this request], but also for [all] those who [will ever] believe and trust in Me through their message . . .[144]

During His "High Priestly Prayer" Jesus demonstrated how to pray for the protection of ourselves, fellow workers of the Gospel, and future believers.

As for me, I love using different versions of the Bible because they reveal various perspectives on how Jesus prayed. Each perspective helps to shape my prayers. Sometimes my prayers are very brief, while other times they are lengthy. In any case, my goal is to follow the pattern and principles that Jesus left for us. With that in mind, let us briefly pray:

---

[143] John 17:15 – Amplified Bible (AMP).

[144] John 17:20 – Amplified Bible (AMP).

Heavenly Father, we adore You for being strong and mighty! You are the King of glory who fights all our battles. Lord, You are "good, a strong hold in the day of trouble; and [You know those who] trust in [You].[145] We need Your help in every area of our lives. We honor Your presence. Thank You for cultivating our thoughts, speech, and actions. Father, we ask in Jesus' name that You will: "Keep us forgiven with you and forgiving others. Keep us safe from ourselves and the Devil. You are in charge! You can do anything you want!"[146] We submit to Your will in Jesus' name. Amen!

---

[145] Nahum 1:7 - King James Version (KJV).

[146] Matthew 6:7-13 - The Message (MSG).

Chapter 9

Practicing the Discipline of Prayer

Following Jesus' blueprint helps to create and maintain an atmosphere of prayer that honors our Father. Being our perfect example, Christ Jesus showed us how transformation takes place in the atmosphere of prayer. Watch the process:

> *[Jesus] climbed the mountain to pray, taking Peter, John, and James along. While He was in prayer, the appearance of His face changed, and His clothes became blinding white. At once two men were there talking with Him. They turned out to be Moses and Elijah—and what a glorious appearance they made! They talked over His exodus; the one Jesus was about to complete in Jerusalem. Meanwhile, Peter and those with Him were slumped over in sleep. When they came to, rubbing their eyes, they saw Jesus in His glory and the two men standing with Him. When Moses and Elijah had left, Peter said to Jesus, "Master, this is a great moment!* [147]

---

[147] Luke 9:28-29 - The Message (MSG).

Learning from Jesus—the children of God can pray effectual, fervent prayers and experience the transforming presence of God.

Through and by the transforming presence of God, unregenerated humans are changed into new creations. 2 Corinthians 3:18 informs,

> . . . when God is personally present, a living Spirit, that old, constricting legislation is recognized as obsolete. We are free of it! All of us! Nothing between us and God, our faces shining with the brightness of His face. And so, we are transfigured much like the Messiah, our lives gradually becoming brighter and more beautiful as God enters our lives and we become like Him. [148]

From a personal perspective, during my new birth, I experienced the transforming power of God in the atmosphere of prayer.

Although I have been transformed into a new creation, I am still experiencing an ongoing transformation. By God's design, every child of God will experience an ongoing transformation until our vile bodies are changed and fashioned like unto Jesus' glorious body. But, in this present life, the children of God are experiencing

---

[148] 2 Corinthians 3:18 - The Message (MSG).

the reality of 2 Corinthians 3:18:

> *. . .we all, with unveiled faces, continually seeing as in a mirror the glory of the Lord, are being progressively transformed into His image from [one degree of] glory to [even more] glory, which comes from the Lord, [who is] the Spirit.*[149]

The Spirit of the Lord is consistently taking the saints of God into greater dimensions of God.

In the process of continuous transformation, the saints of God persistently pray and receive divine revelations, wisdom, greater insight, and healing. Prayer is one of the primary meeting places where God gives believers spiritual blessings. Although God gives divine revelations while we prayerfully study His Word, He is also known for imparting divine revelations during prayer. In any given case, God is the One who "unveils" truths and knowledge about Himself.

When Peter received a divine revelation, Jesus explicitly said,

> *God bless you, Simon, son of Jonah! You did not get that answer out of books or from teachers. My Father*

---

[149] 2 Corinthians 3:18 - Amplified Bible (AMP).

116

in heaven, God Himself, let you in on this secret of
who I really am . . .[150]

While God is known for unveiling truths and knowledge about Himself during and after prayer, He is also known for giving visions.

Interestingly, the same Peter seen in Matthew 16:17 receiving a divine revelation is the same person seen in the book of Acts receiving a vision from God. About the sixth hour, when Peter went up to the housetop to pray,

> *...he fell into a trance. He saw the sky open and a*
> *great canvas sheet, suspended by its four corners,*
> *settle to the ground. In the sheet were all sorts of*
> *animals, snakes, and birds forbidden to the Jews for*
> *food. . .The same vision was repeated three times.*
> *Then the sheet was pulled up again to heaven. . .*
> *Peter was very perplexed. What could the vision*
> *mean? What was he supposed to do? Meanwhile, as*
> *Peter was puzzling over the vision, the Holy Spirit*
> *said to him, "Three men have come to see you. Go*
> *down and meet them and go with them. All is well, I*

---

[150] Matthew 16:17 - The Message (MSG).

have sent them." [151]

Not only did Peter receive a vision, but he also received precise instructions—in the atmosphere of prayer. Furthermore, this same Peter experienced an angelic encounter due to God responding to the prayers of the saints.

While sixteen soldiers guarded Peter in prison, the church was holding a prayer meeting. They prayed effectual fervent prayers for Peter. In response to the prayers of the church, God dispatched an Angel to deliver Peter from prison. At first, Peter thought he was experiencing another vision, possibly because he had preached the prophecy of Joel that spoke of dreams and visions. Nevertheless, when Peter realized he was free, he went directly to the House of Mary.

When Peter arrived at the house of Mary, the mother of John Mark, a prayer meeting was in progress. As seen in the Bible, when the saints of God consistently follow Jesus' pattern and principles for praying effectual fervent prayers, we go "boldly to the very throne of God and stay there to receive His mercy and to find grace to help in our times of need."[152] In response to our prayers, God

---

[151] Acts 10:9-12, 16, 17, 19 & 20 - Living Bible (TLB).

[152] Hebrews 4:16 - Living Bible (TLB).

communicates His plan, reminds us of His unchanging Word, and encourages us to keep practicing the discipline of prayer.

Through continued prayer, Spirit-filled believers will experience the power of the Holy Ghost manifested through dreams, visions, divine revelations, the word of wisdom, the word of knowledge, and prophecies. In addition, there will be an outpouring of the Holy Ghost in the lives of our loved ones, co-workers, friends, and other people from all walks of society.

Holy Ghost Power

In the Old Testament, the Spirit of God anointed chosen individuals such as judges, kings, priests, and prophets. God's chosen ones received the anointing for only a specific incident or time. God anointed them from the time of their calling until they passed from this life. Regardless of the duration of their anointing, the manifestation of God's Spirit in their lives was authentic and supernatural. Although the Spirit of God moved upon the Old Testament saints, humans still long to experience the fulfillment of the Old Testament prophecies regarding the baptism of the Holy Ghost. Beginning with Joel and continuing through John the Baptist, God's prophets foretold of a time when the Spirit of God would reside within humans rather than merely moving upon them.[153]

With the culmination of the Old Testament age, the life and ministry of Jesus transitioned the Old Testament into the New Testament era. Encapsulated in Jesus' overall message was promises concerning the outpouring of the Holy Ghost. John 7:37-39, reveals:

> . . .on the last and most important day of the feast, *Jesus stood and called out [in a loud voice], "If anyone is thirsty, let him come to Me and drink! He who believes in Me [who adheres to, trusts in, and relies on Me], as the Scripture has said, 'From his innermost being will flow continually rivers of living water.'" But He was speaking of the [Holy] Spirit, whom those who believed in Him [as Savior] were to receive afterward. The Spirit had not yet been given, because Jesus was not yet glorified (raised to honor).*[154]

Interestingly, Jesus compared the future coming of the Holy Ghost

---

[153] Isaiah 28:11-12, Isaiah 44:3, Ezekiel 36:27, and Hosea 6:3.

[154] John 7:37-39 - Amplified Bible (AMP).

to having "rivers of water" flowing from our inner being.

Jesus also spoke concerning the promise of the Holy Ghost during His discourse to His disciples in response to their request that He teach them how to pray. After He revealed His pattern for praying, Jesus explained to those present that our Heavenly Father is willing and desires to give good gifts to those who ask of Him. Jesus further stated that everyone who asks for the Holy Ghost will receive it. Furthermore, Luke recorded that just before Jesus' ascension, He stood with an estimated 500 followers on Mount Olivet and instructed them to remain in Jerusalem and wait for the promise of God, which is the Holy Ghost.[155] However, only 120 of them were together praying, praising God, and waiting for the promise.

Acts 2:1-4 reveals the initial fulfillment of the Old Testament prophecies concerning the outpouring of the Holy Ghost, saying:

> *And when the day of Pentecost [fully came], they*
> *were all with one accord in one place. And suddenly*
> *there came a sound from heaven as of a rushing*
> *mighty wind, and it filled all the house where they*

---

[155] Luke 24:49 – King James Version (KJV).

were sitting. And there appeared upon them cloven tongues like as of fire, and it sat upon each of them. And they were all filled with the Holy Ghost, and began to speak with other tongues, as the Spirit gave them utterance.[156]

The book of Acts also gives accounts of the outpouring of the Holy Ghost on the Samaritans and on the Gentiles.[157]

To God be the glory! All because of the finished work of Christ, the Holy Ghost power is for every person who repents during this Grace Age Dispensation. After an individual turns to the one true God, prays the prayer of repentance, is born of the water, and is born of the Spirit, that person shall receive the promise with the evidence of speaking with other tongues as the Holy Ghost gives utterance. By receiving the promise of the Holy Ghost, we become the children of God. In fact, we are citizens of God's Kingdom and can freely use our privilege to build ourselves upon our most holy faith by praying in the Holy Ghost.

---

[156] Acts 2:1-4 - King James Version (KJV).

[157] Reference: Acts 8:14-17 and Acts 10:44-48.

Chapter 10

Conclusion

Jesus is the Master Teacher of praying effectual and fervent prayers. Being the greatest Prayer Warrior, He knows how to navigate the pathway of prayer. Jesus knows the intricate details of how to approach the very throne of God. In fact, He is the way, the truth, and the life needed for having access to God's throne. Through His atoning sacrifice, Jesus bridged the gap between God and humans and made it possible for us to have direct access to God through spiritual adoption. The very moment an individual is adopted into God's family, that person has the privilege to call the infinite God of the universe—Father.

The boundless God of the universe is infinitely omniscient, omnipotent, and omnipresent. Since God is omnipresent, all humans have the privilege to communicate with Him at any time. Since He is omnipotent, He can do whatever He wants to do. He is the King of kings, and He reigns over all the kingdoms of the earth. He is the God of all flesh who knows all the codes, symbols, letters, and words that are used to give meaning to every language. So, right now, wherever you are, you can use your own language and pray to our Creator. Whether you are saved or unsaved, God wants to hear from you.

Gwen E. Brannum

In His infinite wisdom, God knows how to respond to your prayers. For example, if you come to God in faith, seeking to be adopted into His family, and pray the prayer of repentance, He will respond to you. After you fulfill all His prerequisites in faith-filled obedience, God will adopt you into His family. In other words, He will give you the seal of approval for being a citizen of His Kingdom. As a result, you will have the right, privilege, and responsibility to pray in a new dimension. The beauty of it all is that, as a dear child of God, you can pray to the boundless God of the universe, addressing Him as "Abba Father."

When we pray, saying "**Abba Father**," we are, in fact, addressing the infinite source of all existence. In humble adoration, we worship our High and Holy Father for being holy, righteous, and faithful. With hearts filled with adoration, we joyfully pray, "**Our Father who art in Heaven**." At this point, we are honoring Him for being the God of the universe who transcends all space and time. With awe-filled worship, we honor Him for being the Supreme Ruler who gives His children good gifts.

One of the greatest gifts our Father has bestowed upon His children is His name. With the privilege of bearing the name of our Father comes the responsibility to represent His name in royal style. Therefore, we pray, "**May Your Name be honored**." In other words, we pray for wisdom to behave in a manner compatible with our status as children of God. Although we can do nothing to enhance the holiness of God's name, we can certainly honor and bring glory to His name by living a life of sanctification. Honoring our Father's name is more than words; it is a lifestyle.

In honor of our Father's name, our first commitment is to Him and His Kingdom. So, we pray "**May Your Kingdom come**." In this present time, the Kingdom of God has been placed in the hearts of Spirit-filled believers. Now, we are God's ambassadors, and we are sharing the good news that God's Kingdom is accessible through the atoning sacrifice of Jesus Christ. As we endeavor to advance the Kingdom, we pray for God's Kingdom to be established in the hearts of people in every sphere of the marketplace, in our families, in our neighborhoods, as well as in the hearts of people all over the world. In addition, we pray for **God's will to be done on earth as it is in heaven**.

As we continue to follow Jesus' blueprint for praying, we ask our Father to "**Give us our daily bread and to forgive us as we forgive others**." Divine forgiveness is deeply embedded in the story of humanity. Jesus knows the intricate details of humans' propensity to seek revenge for wrongs committed against them. However, He wants us to follow a more charitable way by loving and forgiving others. Furthermore, we ask God to "**Keep us safe from ourselves and the Devil**."

Throughout our prayers, we worship our Father for being in charge. So, as we close each prayer, we pray in this fashion, "**Thine is the kingdom, and the power, and the glory**." In honor of the King of kings, we bow in humble adoration. Also, we thank Him in advance for supplying all our needs, including the supernatural answers He provides. As a result, God gives us peace, and He faithfully provides the necessary strength we need to consistently follow Jesus' blueprint and principles for praying effectual, fervent prayers.

Being our perfect example, Christ Jesus showed us how to experience transformation in the atmosphere of prayer. Through and by the transforming presence of God, unregenerated humans are changed into new creations. 2 Corinthians 3:18 informs us,

> . . . when God is personally present, a living Spirit, that old, constricting legislation is recognized as obsolete. We are free of it! All of us! Nothing between us and God, our faces shining with the brightness of His face. And so, we are transfigured much like the Messiah, our lives gradually becoming brighter and more beautiful as God enters our lives and we

become like Him.[158]

Through continued prayer, Spirit-filled believers will experience the power of the Holy Ghost manifested through dreams, visions, divine revelations, the word of wisdom, the word of knowledge, and prophecies.

In addition, there will be an outpouring of the Holy Ghost in the lives of our loved ones, co-workers, friends, and other people from all walks of society. Also, people will be healed spiritually, mentally, physically, socially, and financially. By God's design, there will be a supernatural increase in every dimension of wealth in the lives of God's people. These are the last days, and God's Word is being fulfilled throughout the world as He continues to transform lives through and by the power of the Holy Ghost.

All because of the finished work of Christ, the Holy Ghost power is for every person who repents during this Grace Age Dispensation. After an individual prays the prayer of repentance, turns to the one true God, is born of the water, and is born of the Spirit, that person shall receive the promise with the evidence of speaking with other tongues as the Holy Ghost gives utterance. By receiving the promise of the Holy Ghost, we become the children of

---

[158] 2 Corinthians 3:18 - The Message (MSG).

God. As a result, we are citizens of God's Kingdom who have the authority, privilege, and responsibility to pray in a new dimension. In fact, we can freely use our privilege to build ourselves upon our most holy faith by praying in the Holy Ghost.

Works Cited

"Amplified Bible (AMP) - - 2 Corinthians 3:18." Bible Gateway, The Lockman Foundation, 2015, www.biblegateway.com. Accessed 15 Aug. 2024.

"Amplified Bible (AMP) - - 1 John 2:16." Bible Gateway, The Lockman Foundation, 2015, www.biblegateway.com. Accessed 15 Aug. 2024.

"Amplified Bible (AMP) - - 1 John 3:1." Bible Gateway, The Lockman Foundation, 2015, www.biblegateway.com. Accessed 10 Oct. 2024.

"Amplified Bible (AMP) - - 1 John 5:14." Bible Gateway, The Lockman Foundation, 2015, www.biblegateway.com. Accessed 31 Dec. 2024.

"Amplified Bible (AMP) - - 1 Peter 2:9, 1 Peter 5:8-9, 2 Peter 3:10-11." Bible Gateway, The Lockman Foundation, 2015, www.biblegateway.com. Accessed 30 Aug. 2024.

"Amplified Bible (AMP) - - Acts 17:28." Bible Gateway, The Lockman Foundation, 2015, www.biblegateway.com. Accessed 10 Jan. 2025.

"Amplified Bible (AMP) - - Ecclesiastes 12:13." Bible Gateway, The Lockman Foundation, 2015, www.biblegateway.com.

Accessed 10 Jul. 2024.

"Amplified Bible (AMP) - - Ephesians 6:16." Bible Gateway, The Lockman Foundation, 2015, www.biblegateway.com. Accessed 10 Jul. 2024.

"Amplified Bible (AMP) - - Exodus 3:1-4, Exodus 3:7-9, Exodus 3:10-12." Bible Gateway, The Lockman Foundation, 2015, www.biblegateway.com. Accessed 23 Nov. 2024.

"Amplified Bible (AMP) - - Galatians 5:22-23." Bible Gateway, The Lockman Foundation, 2015, www.biblegateway.com. Accessed 10 Oct. 2024.

"Amplified Bible (AMP) - - Genesis 2:15-17, Genesis 4:26." Bible Gateway, The Lockman Foundation, 2015, www.biblegateway.com. Accessed 31 Dec. 2024.

"Amplified Bible (AMP) - - Hebrews 12:11." Bible Gateway, The Lockman Foundation, 2015, www.biblegateway.com. Accessed 31 Dec. 2024.

"Amplified Bible (AMP) - - Isaiah 1:4, 6-7, Isaiah 1:18-20." Bible Gateway, The Lockman Foundation, 2015, www.biblegateway.com. Accessed 10 Oct. 2024.

"Amplified Bible (AMP) - - Jeremiah 33:3." Bible Gateway, The Lockman Foundation, 2015, www.biblegateway.com. Accessed 30 Aug. 2024.

"Amplified Bible (AMP) - - John 1:29, John 4:46-53, John 7:37-39." Bible Gateway, The Lockman Foundation, 2015, www.biblegateway.com. Accessed 10 Oct. 2024.

"Amplified Bible (AMP) - - John 11:39-44, John 15:15 & 20." Bible Gateway, The Lockman Foundation, 2015, www.biblegateway.com. Accessed 17 Jan. 2025.

"Amplified Bible (AMP) - - Luke 11:9-10, Luke 17:12-20, Luke 22:44." Bible Gateway, The Lockman Foundation, 2015, www.biblegateway.com. Accessed 14 Jul. 2024.

"Amplified Bible (AMP) - - Mark 11:24, Mark 4:35, Mark 9:22-26." Bible Gateway, The Lockman Foundation, 2015, www.biblegateway.com. Accessed 7 May. 2024.

"Amplified Bible (AMP) - - Matthew 4:1-4, Matthew 6:11-12, 14-15, Matthew 24:35, Matthew 26:42." Bible Gateway, The Lockman Foundation, 2015, www.biblegateway.com. Accessed 10 May. 2024.

"Amplified Bible (AMP) - - Philippians 2:13." Bible Gateway, The Lockman Foundation, 2015, www.biblegateway.com. Accessed 5 May. 2024.

"Amplified Bible (AMP) - - Psalm 8:9, Psalm 29:4, Psalm 37:4." Bible Gateway, The Lockman Foundation, 2015, www.biblegateway.com. Accessed 5 May. 2024.

"Amplified Bible (AMP) - - Revelation 14:2." Bible Gateway, The Lockman Foundation, 2015, www.biblegateway.com. Accessed 23 May. 2024.

"Amplified Bible, Classic Edition (AMPC) - - 2 Timothy 3:3-4." Bible Gateway, The Lockman Foundation, 1987, www.biblegateway.com. Accessed 10 Oct. 2024.

"Darby Translation (DARBY) - - Matthew 4:4." Bible Gateway, Public Domain, 2024, www.biblegateway.com. Accessed 10 Jul. 2024.

"English Standard Version (ESV) - - 1 Kings 19:11-13." Bible Gateway, Crossway Bibles, a publishing ministry of Good News Publishers, 2001, www.biblegateway.com. Accessed 10 Nov. 2024.

"English Standard Version (ESV) - - Daniel 5:5-9." Bible Gateway, Crossway Bibles, a publishing ministry of Good News Publishers, 2001, www.biblegateway.com. Accessed 3 Nov. 2024

"English Standard Version (ESV) - - John 11:41-45." Bible Gateway, Crossway Bibles, a publishing ministry of Good News Publishers, 2001, www.biblegateway.com. Accessed 13 May 2024

"English Standard Version (ESV) - - Matthew 6:31-33." Bible

Gateway, Crossway Bibles, a publishing ministry of Good News Publishers, 2001, www.biblegateway.com. Accessed 10 Oct 2024

"English Standard Version (ESV) - - Numbers 22:21-35." Bible Gateway, Crossway Bibles, a publishing ministry of Good News Publishers, 2001, www.biblegateway.com. Accessed 10 Oct 2024

"God's Word Translation (GW) - - Exodus 2:11-15." Bible Gateway, God's Word to the Nations Mission Society, 2020, www.biblegateway.com. Accessed 17 Jan. 2025.

"Good News Translation (GNT) - - Mark 4:39-41." Bible Gateway, American Bible Society, 1992, www.biblegateway.com. Accessed 14 May. 2024.

"Good News Translation (GNT) - - Matthew 6:9-10." Bible Gateway, American Bible Society, 1992, www.biblegateway.com. Accessed 17 Aug. 2024.

"J.B. Phillips New Testament (PHILLIPS) - - Hebrews 7:24-25, Hebrews 7:26-27." Bible Gateway, The New Testament in Modern English by J.B Phillips, 1972, www.biblegateway.com. Accessed 14 May. 2024.

"King James Version (KJV) - - Acts 2:1-4, Acts 8:14-17, Acts 10:44-48." Bible Gateway, Public Domain, 2025, www.biblegateway.com. Accessed 17 Jan. 2025.

"King James Version (KJV) - - 1 Samuel 3." Bible Gateway, Public Domain, 2024, www.biblegateway.com. Accessed 23 Nov. 2024.

"King James Version (KJV) - - 1 Thessalonians 5:17." Bible Gateway, Public Domain, 2025, www.biblegateway.com. Accessed 17 Jan. 2025.

"King James Version (KJV) - - Exodus 3." Bible Gateway, Public Domain, 2024, www.biblegateway.com. Accessed 23 Nov. 2024.

"King James Version (KJV) - - Genesis 1:28-30." Bible Gateway, Public Domain, 2024, www.biblegateway.com. Accessed 23 Nov. 2024.

"King James Version (KJV) - - Hebrews 4:14-16." Bible Gateway, Public Domain, 2024, www.biblegateway.com. Accessed 10 Oct. 2024.

"King James Version (KJV) - - Jeremiah 33:3." Bible Gateway, Public Domain, 2024, www.biblegateway.com. Accessed 15 Aug. 2024.

"King James Version (KJV) - - John 6:63." Bible Gateway, Public Domain, 2024, www.biblegateway.com. Accessed 15 Aug. 2024.

"King James Version (KJV) - - John 14:6." Bible Gateway, Public Domain, 2024, www.biblegateway.com. Accessed 30 Aug. 2024.

"King James Version (KJV) - - John 17:11." Bible Gateway, Public Domain, 2025, www.biblegateway.com. Accessed 17 Jan. 2025.

"King James Version (KJV) - - Jonah 1-4." Bible Gateway, Public Domain, 2024, www.biblegateway.com. Accessed 10 Oct. 2024.

"King James Version (KJV) - - Judges 6." Bible Gateway, Public Domain, 2024, www.biblegateway.com. Accessed 23 Nov. 2024.

"King James Version (KJV) - - Isaiah 58:1." Bible Gateway, Public Domain, 2024, www.biblegateway.com. Accessed 23 Nov. 2024.

"King James Version (KJV) - - James 1:15." Bible Gateway, Public Domain, 2024, www.biblegateway.com. Accessed 31 Dec. 2024.

"King James Version (KJV) - - John 12:27-38." Bible Gateway, Public Domain, 2024, www.biblegateway.com. Accessed 25 Dec. 2024.

"King James Version (KJV) - - Luke 23:34." Bible Gateway, Public

Domain, 2025, www.biblegateway.com. Accessed 10 Jan. 2025.

King James Version (KJV) - - Luke 24:49." Bible Gateway, Public Domain, 2025, www.biblegateway.com. Accessed 17 Jan. 2025.

"King James Version (KJV) - - Mark 15:34." Bible Gateway, Public Domain, 2024, www.biblegateway.com. Accessed 23 Nov. 2024.

"King James Version (KJV) - - Matthew 3:13-17, Matthew 6:13." Bible Gateway, Public Domain, 2024, www.biblegateway.com. Accessed 10 Oct. 2024.

"King James Version (KJV) - - Matthew 7:24-29" Bible Gateway, Public Domain, 2023, www.biblegateway.com. Accessed 10 Oct. 2024.

"King James Version (KJV) - - Matthew 11:25-26." Bible Gateway, Public Domain, 2024, www.biblegateway.com. Accessed 10 Oct. 2024.

"King James Version (KJV) - - Matthew 15:36, Matthew 26:36-46." Bible Gateway, Public Domain, 2024, www.biblegateway.com. Accessed 10 Oct. 2024.

"King James Version (KJV) - - Mark 1:9-11." Bible Gateway, Public Domain, 2024, www.biblegateway.com. Accessed 15

Aug. 2024.

"King James Version (KJV) - - Mark 4:35, 37-38." Bible Gateway, Public Domain, 2024, www.biblegateway.com. Accessed 10 Jul. 2024.

"King James Version (KJV) - - Mark 7:24-29." Bible Gateway, Public Domain, 2024, www.biblegateway.com. Accessed 10 Jul. 2024.

"King James Version (KJV) - - Mark 14:36." Bible Gateway, Public Domain, 2024, www.biblegateway.com. Accessed 23 Nov. 2024.

"King James Version (KJV) - - Nahum 1:7." Bible Gateway, Public Domain, 2025, www.biblegateway.com. Accessed 17 Jan. 2025.

"King James Version (KJV) - - Psalm 115:3." Bible Gateway, Public Domain, 2024, www.biblegateway.com. Accessed 15 Aug. 2024.

"King James Version (KJV) - - Luke 3:21-23." Bible Gateway, Public Domain, 2024, www.biblegateway.com. Accessed 10 Oct. 2024.

"King James Version (KJV) - - 1 Peter 5:7." Bible Gateway, Public Domain, 2024, www.biblegateway.com. Accessed 30 Aug. 2024.

Gwen E. Brannum

"King James Version (KJV) - - 1 Samuel 3." Bible Gateway, Public Domain, 2024, www.biblegateway.com. Accessed 30 Aug. 2024.

"King James Version (KJV) - - 1 Thessalonians 5:17." Bible Gateway, Public Domain, 2024, www.biblegateway.com. Accessed 7 May. 2024.

"King James Version (KJV) - - Exodus 3." Bible Gateway, Public Domain, 2024, www.biblegateway.com. Accessed 10 Oct. 2024.

"King James Version (KJV) - - Isaiah 58:1." Bible Gateway, Public Domain, 2024, www.biblegateway.com. Accessed 10 Oct. 2024.

"King James Version (KJV) - - James 1:15." Bible Gateway, Public Domain, 2024, www.biblegateway.com. Accessed 31 Dec. 2024.

"King James Version (KJV) - - John 14:6." Bible Gateway, Public Domain, 2024, www.biblegateway.com. Accessed 23 Dec. 2024.

"King James Version (KJV) - - John 6:63b." Bible Gateway, Public Domain, 2024, www.biblegateway.com. Accessed 5 oct. 2024.

"King James Version (KJV) - - Jonah 1-4." Bible Gateway, Public

Domain, 2024, www.biblegateway.com. Accessed 5 oct. 2024.

"King James Version (KJV) - - Judges 6." Bible Gateway, Public Domain, 2024, www.biblegateway.com. Accessed 3 May. 2024.

"King James Version (KJV) - - Luke 1:13-17, Luke 1:30-37, and Luke 2:9-14, Luke 23:34, 46." Bible Gateway, Public Domain, 2024, www.biblegateway.com. Accessed 3 Dec. 2024.

"King James Version (KJV) - - Mark 4:37-3." Bible Gateway, Public Domain, 2024, www.biblegateway.com. Accessed 3 Dec. 2024.

"King James Version (KJV) - - Matthew 15:36" Bible Gateway, Public Domain, 2024, www.biblegateway.com. Accessed 3 Dec. 2024.

"King James Version (KJV) - - Matthew 11:25-26." Bible Gateway, Public Domain, 2024, www.biblegateway.com. Accessed 3 Dec. 2024.

"King James Version (KJV) - - Matthew 6:13." Bible Gateway, Public Domain, 2024, www.biblegateway.com. Accessed 15 Aug. 2024.

"King James Version (KJV) - - Matthew 7:24-29." Bible Gateway,

Public Domain, 2024, www.biblegateway.com. Accessed 10 May. 2024.

"King James Version (KJV) - - Psalm 20:1." Bible Gateway, Public Domain, 2024, www.biblegateway.com. Accessed 4 Jul. 2024.

"King James Version (KJV) - - Psalm 46:1." Bible Gateway, Public Domain, 2024, www.biblegateway.com. Accessed 30 Aug. 2024.

"King James Version (KJV) - - Psalm 90:1-2." Bible Gateway, Public Domain, 2024, www.biblegateway.com. Accessed 30 Aug. 2024.

"King James Version (KJV) - - Psalm 100:5." Bible Gateway, Public Domain, 2024, www.biblegateway.com. Accessed 4 Jul. 2024.

"King James Version (KJV) - - Romans 12:2." Bible Gateway, Public Domain, 2024, www.biblegateway.com. Accessed 10 Aug. 2024.

"King James Version (KJV) - - Romans 13:14." Bible Gateway, Public Domain, 2024, www.biblegateway.com. Accessed 3 Aug. 2024.

"Living Bible (TLB) - - Acts 10:9-12, 16, 17, 19 & 20." Bible Gateway, Thomas Nelson, 1982, www.biblegateway.com.

Accessed 15 Aug. 2024.

"Living Bible (TLB) - - Hebrews 1:1." Bible Gateway, Thomas Nelson, 1982, www.biblegateway.com. Accessed 15 Aug. 2024.

"Living Bible (TLB) - - Hebrews 11:1." Bible Gateway, Thomas Nelson, 1982, www.biblegateway.com. Accessed 15 Aug. 2024.

"Living Bible (TLB) - - Hebrews 4:12." Bible Gateway, Thomas Nelson, 1982, www.biblegateway.com. Accessed 10 Jul. 2024.

"Living Bible (TLB) - - Hebrews 4:16." Bible Gateway, Thomas Nelson, 1982, www.biblegateway.com. Accessed 10 Jul. 2024.

"Living Bible (TLB) - - John 17:15-17." Bible Gateway, Thomas Nelson, 1982, www.biblegateway.com. Accessed 10 Jan. 2025.

"Living Bible (TLB) - - Luke 18:1." Bible Gateway, Thomas Nelson, 1982, www.biblegateway.com. Accessed 10 Jul. 2024.

"Living Bible (TLB) - - Luke 6:12-13." Bible Gateway, Thomas Nelson, 1982, www.biblegateway.com. Accessed 10 Jul. 2024.

"Living Bible (TLB) - - Mark 7:24-29." Bible Gateway, Thomas Nelson, 1982, www.biblegateway.com. Accessed 10 Dec. 2024.

"Living Bible (TLB) - - Matthew 26:39." Bible Gateway, Thomas Nelson, 1982, www.biblegateway.com. Accessed 10 Dec. 2024.

"Living Bible (TLB) - - Philippians 4:6-9." Bible Gateway, Thomas Nelson, 1982, www.biblegateway.com. Accessed 10 Dec. 2024.

"Living Bible (TLB) - - Philippians 4:7." Bible Gateway, Thomas Nelson, 1982, www.biblegateway.com. Accessed 15 Aug. 2024.

"New International Version (NIV) - - Colossians 3:17." Bible Gateway, Public Domain, 2024, www.biblegateway.com. Accessed 13 Nov. 2024.

"New International Version (NIV) - - Exodus 4:11." Bible Gateway, Public Domain, 2024, www.biblegateway.com. Accessed 13 Nov. 2024.

"New International Version (NIV) - - Isaiah 55:6-7." Bible Gateway, Public Domain, 2024, www.biblegateway.com. Accessed 13 Nov. 2024.

"New International Version (NIV) - - Isaiah 55:8-9." Bible Gateway,

Public Domain, 2024, www.biblegateway.com. Accessed 13 Nov. 2024.

"New International Version (NIV) - - Isaiah 55:10-11." Bible Gateway, Public Domain, 2024, www.biblegateway.com. Accessed 13 Nov. 2024.

"New International Version (NIV) - - James 5:17-18." Bible Gateway, Public Domain, 2024, www.biblegateway.com. Accessed 13 Nov. 2024.

"New International Version (NIV) - - Job 38:1." Bible Gateway, Public Domain, 2024, www.biblegateway.com. Accessed 13 Nov. 2024.

"New International Version (NIV) - - Luke 11:1." Bible Gateway, Public Domain, 2024, www.biblegateway.com. Accessed 13 Nov. 2024.

"New International Version (NIV) - - Luke 3:21-22." Bible Gateway, Public Domain, 2024, www.biblegateway.com. Accessed 3 May. 2024.

"New International Version (NIV) - - Mark 1:35." Bible Gateway, Public Domain, 2024, www.biblegateway.com. Accessed 3 May. 2024.

"New International Version (NIV) - - Matthew 9:28." Bible Gateway, Public Domain, 2024, www.biblegateway.com.

Accessed 7 Oct. 2024.

"New International Version (NIV) - - Matthew 9:29-30." Bible Gateway, Public Domain, 2024, www.biblegateway.com. Accessed 30 Aug. 2024.

"New International Version (NIV) - - Matthew 14:22-23." Bible Gateway, Public Domain, 2024, www.biblegateway.com. Accessed 7 Oct. 2024.

"New International Version (NIV) - - Proverbs 4:23." Bible Gateway, Public Domain, 2024, www.biblegateway.com. Accessed 13 Nov. 2024.

"New International Version (NIV) - - 2 Corinthians 5:7." Bible Gateway, Public Domain, 2024, www.biblegateway.com. Accessed 15 Aug. 2024.

"New International Version (NIV) - - Matthew 6:11-12." Bible Gateway, Public Domain, 2024, www.biblegateway.com. Accessed 31 Dec. 2024.

"New International Version (NIV) - - Genesis 1:26-27." Bible Gateway, Public Domain, 2024, www.biblegateway.com. Accessed 31 Dec. 2024.

"New International Version (NIV) - - Psalm 33:9." Bible Gateway, Public Domain, 2024, www.biblegateway.com. Accessed 23 Nov. 2024.

"New Life Version (NLV) - - Matthew 6:11-12." Bible Gateway, Barbour Publishing, Inc., 2024, www.biblegateway.com. Accessed 23 Nov. 2024.

"New Living Translation (NLT) - - Genesis 1:26-27." Bible Gateway, Tyndale House Foundation. 2015, www.biblegateway.com. Accessed 17 Jan. 2025.

"New Living Translation (NLT) - - Psalm 33:9." Bible Gateway, Tyndale House Foundation. 2015, www.biblegateway.com. Accessed 17 Jan. 2025.

"The Living Bible (TLB) - - Hebrews 1:1." Bible Gateway, Tyndale House Foundation. 2003, www.biblegateway.com. Accessed 17 Jan. 2025.

"The Message (MSG) - - 2 Timothy 3:16-17." Bible Gateway, Eugene H. Peterson, 2018, www.biblegateway.com. Accessed 7 May. 2024.

"The Message (MSG) - - Luke 9:28-29." Bible Gateway, Eugene H. Peterson, 2018, www.biblegateway.com. Accessed 23 Nov. 2024.

"The Message (MSG) - - 2 Corinthians 3:18." Bible Gateway, Eugene H. Peterson, 2018, www.biblegateway.com. Accessed 10 Nov. 2024.

"The Message (MSG) - - Job 33:14-18, 18." Bible Gateway, Eugene

H. Peterson, 2018, www.biblegateway.com. Accessed 13 Nov. 2024.

"The Message (MSG) - - Matthew 6:7-13, Matthew 16:17." Bible Gateway, Eugene H. Peterson, 2018, www.biblegateway.com. Accessed 8 Dec. 2024.

About The Author

Dr. Gwen E. Brannum is an advocate of education, and she is committed to being a lifelong student. After graduating from high school in Detroit, Michigan, she has continued her educational journey by attending community colleges, universities, technical institutions, Bible colleges, and seminary. As a result, Dr. Brannum has gained a wealth of insight both spiritually and naturally. From a spiritual perspective, she has received an Associate of Theology, a Bachelor of Science in Biblical Studies, a Master of Arts in Christian Education, a Doctor of Ministry in Christian Counseling, and a Doctor of Philosophy in Christian Business.

Dr. Brannum is also an entrepreneur and humanitarian. As an entrepreneur, she has founded various organizations including Apostolic Pentecostal Truth Ministry, Inc. (1992), Apostolic Pentecostal Truth Ministries, Inc. (2005), Gwen Brannum Ministries, LLC. (2005), Proven to Succeed Ministries, Inc. (2011), Proven to Succeed Day Care, Inc. (2011), and Proven to Succeed Child Development Center, Inc. (2015) - in honor of the boundless Master Builder. As a Christian business owner, Dr. Brannum declares the key to her success is adhering to – *The Master Builder's Blueprint for Building Enduring Wealth* and *Following Jesus' Blueprint for Praying Effectual Fervent Prayers*.

www.ingramcontent.com/pod-product-compliance
Lightning Source LLC
Chambersburg PA
CBHW071754120626
46550CB00002B/792